SPIRIT OF THE LIVING GOD

SPIRIT OF
THE LIVING GOD

LEON MORRIS

INTER-VARSITY PRESS

© INTER-VARSITY PRESS

Inter-Varsity Fellowship
39 Bedford Square, London WC1B 3EY

First Edition	*September 1960*
Reprinted	*December 1961*
Reprinted	*July 1967*
Reprinted	*June 1969*
Reprinted	*April 1972*

ISBN 0 85110 359 6

Printed in Great Britain by
COMPTON PRINTING LIMITED
London and Aylesbury

CONTENTS

PREFACE

THIS little book seeks to set out what seem to me to be some of the important teachings of the Bible on the Holy Spirit, and to do it in a non-technical way for the general reader. In doing this I have tried to avoid two extremes. On the one hand there are scholarly books which set forth much information about the Spirit with many a learned footnote, but which leave the reader wondering in the end, 'What has all this to do with me?' They do not tell him how he may appropriate the Spirit's gifts or what he may expect if he does. At the other extreme are books which avowedly set out to lead the reader into deeper experience. These often tend to regard the Holy Spirit as a more than useful adjunct to the Christian. They show no sign of realizing the majesty of the Spirit's Person, and picture Him as a means of enabling men to lead the godly life. I have tried to steer a middle course between these extremes. I have attempted to show that the Spirit is an awe-inspiring and glorious Figure. He is to be worshipped in His own right as God. But I have tried not to overlook the necessity of giving guidance to those young in the faith as to how they may appropriate the gifts of the Spirit. For it is an obvious fact that, whereas the New Testament speaks appreciably often about being filled with the Spirit, many Christians today give little evidence of the Spirit's power in their lives. It is devoutly to be wished that a practising knowledge of this doctrine should become more widespread. In the hope that it may help just a little to bring about that end this small book goes forth.

LEON MORRIS

CHAPTER I

BORN OF THE SPIRIT

THE Pharisee was a gentleman and a scholar. If he was a trifle condescending towards the Teacher from Galilee he tried hard not to show it. He addressed Him courteously.

'Rabbi,' he began, though he knew that Jesus was not really a Rabbi. He had no diploma. He had never been to the schools. He had not attached Himself to a master. But He was a teacher, so the Pharisee stretched a point. After all, courtesy costs nothing—provided one's associates don't know! 'Rabbi,' he said, 'we know that it is from God you have come as a teacher.' That ought to please Him. There is nothing like showing that you believe a man has divine authorization for what he is saying, especially if you believe it is true.

So Nicodemus the Pharisee began. He had come by night. Was that because he was afraid to come by day when men might see him and label him as a follower of the Nazarene? Possibly. Some scholars are timid souls. If this is the explanation, it is not without interest that Jesus accepted him without rebuke. It is better to come timidly than not to come at all.

Or was it because he thought that in the day there would be crowds? There would be jostling and pushing and thronging. There would be the common people with all their elementary needs and foolish questions. There would be no chance at all of a leisurely talk. But at night Jesus would be much freer. They would be able to sit back and take things easy. Possibly this is the answer, for many scholars are leisurely souls.

Jesus prefixed His opening words with an Aramaic expression which we conveniently translate 'Verily, verily'. I do not know what, if anything, that conveys to the ordinary Englishman (or, for that matter, Australian, Scot, Irishman or American) of the twentieth century. But on Jesus' lips it signified that the following words were especially solemn and

serious, that Jesus placed stress on them, and often also that
they were not what might have been expected and would
therefore require close attention.

'Verily, verily, I say unto thee' runs the preamble; then,
abruptly, 'except a man be born again, he cannot see the
kingdom of God'. Clearly Jesus was in no mood for scholarly
niceties or the pleasantries of polite society. He completely
ignored Nicodemus' opening gambit. He went straight to the
heart of the matter.

Nicodemus should have been at home with the last expression, 'the kingdom of God'. Though the actual words do not
seem to occur in Jewish literature of the period before the
New Testament, the idea is there. For the Jew it was an obvious and basic fact that God reigns. He is supreme in heaven
and the affairs of men. And in His wisdom and His sovereign
choice He has made Israel His own peculiar people. So far
the reasoning was easy. But for centuries (with a brief excep-
tion during the glorious interlude of freedom in the Macca-
bean period) the Jews had been under the heel of the con-
queror, in fact under the heels of a succession of conquerors.
How could this be reconciled with the ideas of the sovereignty
of God and of the Jewish nation as the people of God?

That was not at all easy. But patriotism and piety blended
to produce the fervent (not to say fervid) hope that God
would raise up an outstanding figure who would lead the
down-trodden nation to a striking victory over the hated
Romans. God's own kingdom would be established, with its
capital at Jerusalem and its sway extending over all mankind.
The expectation of the coming of the kingdom was deep and
widespread through Judaism of the time. Nicodemus would
have no difficulty in picking up the allusion.

But the reference to being born again was more difficult.
Incidentally, it is not quite certain that the adverb should be
rendered 'again'. It can mean 'from above', and many translate it this way here. (Barclay attempts to get the best of both
worlds by rendering 'reborn from above'!) But born again
or born from above, what could it mean? Nicodemus did not
know.

So he asked, 'How can a man be born when he is old?' The thing is a physical impossibility. To bring this out he proceeds, 'Can he enter the second time into his mother's womb, and be born?' Now although Jesus' words are difficult, I do not think they are as difficult as all that. It did not take a scholar to discern that He was not talking about anything physical. The statement is clearly metaphorical. Entering into the womb has nothing to do with it at all. Why, then, did Nicodemus choose to make this remark?

Perhaps because he did not like the way the conversation was going. He was a cultured Pharisee, a religious leader. His attainments ought to have been recognized. It was surely not too much to expect that the lowly Teacher from Galilee should have been decently grateful that such a great man should consult Him. Instead He looked dangerously like classing him with the irreligious masses, and requiring of him, the Pharisee, the same kind of 'conversion' that was appropriate to them. So he chose to misunderstand the remark altogether.

But I like to think that Nicodemus was wistful rather than obtuse. A man, he may have been thinking, a man is the sum of all his yesterdays. He is the man he is today because of all the experiences he has had in the past, and because of his reaction to them. He is a bundle of successes and failures, of foolishnesses, of bad habits, of sins, negligences and ignorances, of work and play, of sorrows and joys, of friendships, affections and lusts and wishes and hopes and fears, and all the rest of those complicated things that go to make up human life. It would be wonderful for him to cut loose from all that is bad and limiting. It would be a priceless gift, a good to be coveted above all other goods, to be born again. But it is quite unthinkable for physical birth to be repeated (it has only to be mentioned to be seen for the utter impossibility it is). And why should we think that moral and spiritual rebirth is any easier? How can a man's past possibly be blotted out? To be born again would be magnificent. But . . .

Jesus' response is to repeat His earlier statement with emphasis. Again comes the 'Verily, verily, I say unto thee'.

This is important, Nicodemus. Do not brush it aside or dismiss it as preposterous. 'Except a man be born of water and the Spirit' (notice the change from 'born again' in the previous formulation of this truth), 'he cannot enter into the kingdom of God.'

There have been many attempts to explain what being born 'of water' means. They divide for the most part into three classes. One of them sees a reference to such a rite of purification as that of John the Baptist—a baptism in water for cleansing from sin. If this is the way of understanding it, the meaning will be that a man must repent of his sins. He must be purified from his wicked way. A second possibility rests on a Jewish usage of 'water', 'dew', 'drop' and the like to refer to the male semen. This yields us two alternative ways of understanding our passage. 'Born of water' may be 'born of natural birth'. This is not enough, so a man must also be born 'of the spirit'. Or, 'of water' and 'of the spirit' may be taken very closely together. This will give such a meaning as 'born of spiritual seed', 'born by an activity of the Spirit'. The third class of interpretations sees a reference in some way to the water of Christian baptism. The meaning then would be that a man must be baptized and also be born spiritually if he would enter the kingdom.

There is no point in going deeply into these various possibilities. Possibly more than one is in mind. But for various reasons it seems to me that the most likely solution is that which sees a reference to being born by an activity of the Spirit. Jesus' meaning is something like this: 'I am speaking most solemnly. Do not disregard this. It is, as you imply, quite impossible for a man to enter the womb of his mother for a second time and be born. But for all that a man *must* be reborn. This, I grant, is not a human possibility. But then I am not speaking about a human possibility. I am speaking about an activity of the Spirit of God.'

That this is the correct interpretation of our Lord's words is made clear by what follows. 'That which is born of the flesh,' Jesus went on, 'is flesh; and that which is born of the Spirit is spirit. Don't be astonished that I said to you, "You must be reborn". The wind blows where it wants to' (did they hear a gust of wind howling round the building at that moment?) 'and you hear the noise of it. But you don't know where it's coming from, nor where it's going to. It's like that with everyone who is born of the Spirit' (notice that this time Jesus speaks only of being born 'of the Spirit'; there is no mention of water, which strengthens the opinion that the primary reference in the earlier statement is to the activity of the Spirit).

The stress here is on supernatural activity. Jesus is not talking about anything to do with the flesh. He is talking about an activity of the Spirit. This is as unpredictable by man as the movements of the wind. You can hear the wind and know that there is such a thing. But that does not mean that you are in a position to describe its origin or destination. Being born again is like that. It is not within men's power. They may know that it occurs. But how it is brought about, and where the Spirit-born is being led, they do not know.

Poor Nicodemus is out of his depth. 'How is it possible for these things to take place?' he inquires. And with this plaintive expression of perplexity he vanishes from the narrative. Nothing more is recorded of his end of the conversation. But it is not the last we hear of him, for later on we find him in the number of Christ's followers. Though he was puzzled by this first contact with the mysteries of the new birth, he was not repelled. He followed on until he did come to know for himself what it was all about.

But as yet this was all future. He expresses himself as puzzled. Did Jesus smile, I wonder, as He rejoined, 'You, the teacher of Israel, and you do not know these things?' And then comes a word of reassurance. 'In solemn truth I tell you' ('verily, verily' for the third time in this short conversation), 'we know what we're talking about. We testify to the thing we've seen.' Jesus wants there to be no doubt about the important truth He is enunciating. He is not giving Nicodemus a few seed thoughts on which he may profitably reflect, sifting them to find what are true and what are not. He is speaking the truth about things He knows.

But Jesus is under no illusion as to the reception His good news commonly receives. 'And you don't receive our testimony!' You, Nicodemus, and men like you, do not believe us when we speak definitely of things about which we have certain knowledge. 'If I told you about earthly things and you didn't believe, how will you believe if I tell you about heavenly things?' And with heaven firmly brought into the conversation the Lord proceeds to speak briefly about entrance to that blessed abode. 'No man has ever yet gained the heights of heaven, except him that came down from heaven—the Son of man. And just as Moses lifted the serpent up in the waste lands, so must the Son of man be lifted up, so that everyone who believes may have eternal life in him.'

It is most important to be clear on the point that no man has ever gained heaven by his own effort. Jesus came down that He might raise men to heaven, but that is another matter. It is basic to the present discussion that heaven is for ever unattainable by human effort. That was the error of Nicodemus. He and the rest of the Pharisees like him thought that by their keeping of the Law they were earning a reward with God, and meriting heaven in their own right. Not a bit of it, says Jesus in effect. It is quite impossible for men to attain heaven by anything that they do. They attain it, if they attain it at all, because the Son of man (His favourite title for Himself) came to draw them thither.

And that brings Him immediately to the cost. Long ago, in the wilderness country, in a plague of fiery serpents Moses had made a serpent of brass and put it on a pole. Then those who were bitten by the serpents and who looked in faith to the symbol in brass were cured. The serpent was lifted up on high. The cure came as an act of God's free grace. Jesus will die for men by being lifted up on high on a cross. And whoever looks to Him in faith will receive salvation as an act of God's free grace.

The whole passage stresses over and over, with different pieces of imagery, the thought that man's salvation does not originate with any human device. It is divine in origin and divine in execution. It comes about only as the result of an activity of God. A man must be 'born of the Spirit'.

What does this mean? Why does Jesus speak in this way? Nicodemus was learned in the Old Testament, but he found the teaching strange. What was there which represented an advance on the teaching in those ancient Scriptures? Why, at this time, could Jesus speak of such an activity of the Spirit? What may we know about the ministry of the Spirit? During the rest of this book we shall try to find an answer to some of these questions.

CHAPTER II

THE SPIRIT OF THE LORD

NICODEMUS had read of the Spirit of the Lord in his Bible (our Old Testament), and what is said there must have shaped his thinking as he reflected on Jesus' words about the Spirit. Let us accordingly look briefly at the Old Testament teaching on the Spirit.

THE HEBREW *RUACH*

One of the difficulties that confronts translators from almost any ancient language is that the words for 'spirit', 'breath', and 'wind' are identical. The ancients well understood that a man's breath and wind are much the same. Wind is simply on a large scale what breath is on a small scale. Moreover, breath to most of them seemed something non-material, something intangible. And when a man died his breath ceased. When they began to think of a spirit within man, small wonder that they used the same word as that for 'breath' to denote it. Alternatively, they thought of breath as material, but those who did so also thought of man's spirit as material in the same way. The end product is the same. 'Breath', 'wind' and 'spirit' may all be denoted by one word.

All this is very understandable, but that does not make it any easier to translate an ancient document. When we meet a word which has these various meanings, which one are we to choose? The decision is sometimes far from easy.

In Hebrew the word *ruach*, which we usually render 'spirit', is not the only word for 'breath'. There is also *neshamah*. The difference between them appears to be that *neshamah* denotes ordinary quiet breathing, while *ruach* signifies heavy breathing. There is often the notion of violence. N. Snaith gives the meaning of this root as 'to breathe out through the nose with violence', and he adds, 'It is an onomatopoetic word'.[1] *Ruach* and *neshamah* sometimes appear as synonyms, but this is when the essential meanings are not involved. If we may liken the meaning of a word to a circle, then the circles representing *ruach* and *neshamah* overlap a little out towards the circumferences. But their centres, their inner characteristic meanings, are well apart. Where the distinctive significance of *ruach* appears we get the thought of violence, or of power. There are, for example, a number of passages where the word means 'wind'. Thus in Exodus x. 19 we read of 'an exceeding strong west wind'.[2] In Exodus xv. 8 a similar wind is referred to with the same Hebrew word, but this time it is translated 'the blast of thy nostrils'. In Psalm cxlviii. 8 and Ezekiel i. 4, it is a 'stormy wind' (in the Ezekiel passage AV has 'a whirlwind'); in Isaiah xxv. 4 'the blast of the terrible ones'; while in Isaiah xxx. 28 God's 'breath' is likened to 'an overflowing stream'. Much more could be quoted. It is plain that the throbbing note of power characterizes *ruach*.

When the term is used of a man it will not surprise us that it is the dominant part of man that is meant. Snaith brings out the force of *ruach* in man with a brief discussion of its use in Genesis xxvi. 35. This passage 'states that the two Hittite wives of Esau were "bitterness of spirit" (*morath ruach*) to Isaac and Rebekah. The RV "grief of mind" is inadequate. The meaning is that whenever they thought of these marriages of Esau, the feeling which dominated them was one of bitterness and this to the exclusion of every other feeling. An overwhelming sense of bitterness came upon them.'[3] When Hosea complained of 'the spirit of whoredom' (v. 4) he was not referring to an occasional scandal. He meant that the dominant attitude of the people was wayward. Ezekiel speaks of 'a new heart and a new spirit' (Ezk. xviii. 31), which points to the renewal of the whole inner life of man, of the essential part of man, and not anything of less importance.

---

[1] *The Distinctive Ideas of the Old Testament*, London, 1950, p. 143.

[2] Unless otherwise stated, references from this point onwards are from the RV.

[3] *Op. cit.*, p. 146.

THE ALL-POWERFUL SPIRIT

Passages like these prepare us for the thought that when *ruach* is used of God it points to Him as completely irresistible, as strong in might. It usually denotes God in action, and His action inevitably accomplishes that which He pleases. There are other aspects of God. He is Majestic. He may sometimes be discerned in the quiet rather than in the storm (1 Ki. xix. 11f.). But such aspects are not in mind when 'the Spirit of the Lord' is used. Then we think of God in vigorous action, of God doing something that cannot be withstood.

This meaning of *ruach*, paradoxically enough, is made clear by a number of passages in which the meaning is not quite certain. Here we must notice a peculiarity of Hebrew, namely that it has no superlative. There is nothing corresponding to the '—est' termination in English. When the Hebrews wished to convey this idea they had to do it some other way. For example, in Judges v. 24 we read that Jael shall be 'blessed above women', where the Hebrew actually reads 'blessed *from* women'. That is to say, in the matter of blessedness Jael stands apart 'from' other women, Jael will be the most blessed of all women.

Another way of expressing such a thought is by referring to heaven or to God. Thus the cities of the Canaanites are said to be 'great and fenced up to heaven' (Dt. ix. 1). But the Hebrews did not really think that these town walls touched the sky. It was their way of saying that the walls were 'very high'. So when we read in Genesis x. 9 that Nimrod was 'a mighty hunter before the Lord', this means that Nimrod was the mightiest of hunters. If he was mighty even before the Lord, what must he have been before men?

A *ruach YHWH*, 'a wind of the Lord' (see Is. xl. 7), will, if it is an example of this construction, mean 'a very strong wind', i.e. a wind that is a wind even to God! Yet if we wanted to say in Hebrew 'the Spirit of the Lord', we would have to use exactly the same Hebrew expression. A very interesting illustration of the problems that may be posed by this construction is seen in Isaiah lix. 19, where AV translates by 'the Spirit of the Lord', while Moffatt renders 'a blast of wind'. Who is to say which is right?

There is no need to pursue this aspect of our subject further. It is clear that *ruach* denotes something mighty. When it is used of God there is the thought of His irresistibility. The Spirit of the Lord lifts men up and transports them where He will (2 Ki. ii. 16; Ezk. iii. 14, etc.). The Spirit of the Lord acts with the power of a mighty wind. Man cannot resist Him.

COSMIC AFFAIRS

Since 'the Spirit' directs attention to the power of God, it is not surprising that the Spirit is mentioned in Genesis i as active in creation. 'The Spirit of God moved upon the face of the waters' (Gn. i. 2) might be rendered 'the Spirit of God brooded over the waters'. The figure is that of a bird hovering over its young. The Spirit was present in creative power. G. J. Spurrell aptly cites Milton's *Paradise Lost* as giving the meaning of the passage:

> 'His brooding wings the Spirit of God outspread,
> And vital virtue infused, and vital warmth
> Throughout the fluid mass.'[1]

God's Spirit was active in bringing to pass the ordered universe.

The thought is not common in the Old Testament (though it does recur; for example, in Job xxxiii. 4 we read, 'The spirit of God hath made me', and in Job xxvi. 13, 'By his spirit the heavens are garnished'). But everywhere it is assumed that it is by God that all things were created. And the Spirit is commonly used to express the thought of God in action.

THE GIVER OF LIFE

Life is such a significant part of creation that it deserves a section to itself. The Spirit is active in creating all things, but the Old Testament associates the Spirit especially with the origin of life. Thus 'the Lord God formed man of the dust

[1] *Notes on the Hebrew Text of the Book of Genesis*, Oxford, 1887, p. 5.

of the ground', but it was only when He 'breathed into his nostrils the breath of life' that 'man became a living soul' (Gn. ii. 7). The term 'Spirit' (*ruach*) does not occur here, but it is surely implied. Life in man comes only from God's Spirit.[1]

A little puzzle is presented now and then by a reference to 'the breath (*ruach*) of God'. Does this mean the life that is in man, considered as God-given breath? Or does it point to an activity of God's Spirit?

There is a striking example in Ezekiel's story of the valley of dry bones (Ezk. xxxvii. 1–14). In his vision the prophet sees himself carried away to a valley full of dry bones. He expressly comments, 'lo, they were very dry'. He is asked whether such bones can live, and will not commit himself on the point: God alone has knowledge of such things. Then he is commanded to prophesy over the bones. As he does so, there is a noise and a movement, and before his very eyes the bones which have been scattered come together. Then sinews and flesh appear, and skin covers them. But up till this point there is no alteration in the most significant fact of all—the bones are the bones of dead men.

But now the prophet is bidden to prophesy to 'the wind' (or 'breath' or 'spirit'; which is it?). He does so. The breath comes into them. And before the prophet's astonished gaze they stand up on their feet, 'an exceeding great army'.

There is not the slightest doubt about the meaning of this. It is only as the Spirit of God brings life that there can be life. The precise application of the vision is to the Israelites at the time of the exile. Their nation was dead. They were men without hope. They saw no way of restoration. They were as good as in their graves. But the Lord promises that He will bring the nation to life again. He will open their very graves and bring those dead men out. He says, 'I will put my spirit in you, and ye shall live' (Ezk. xxxvii. 14). The Spirit of the Lord means life.

---

[1] Cf. H. E. Ryle, man's life 'is not the product of his body, but the gift of God's breath or spirit' (*Cambridge Bible for Schools and Colleges, in loc.*).

In similar fashion Job can speak of his life and of the Spirit of God as being much the same thing: 'For my life is yet whole in me, and the spirit of God is in my nostrils' (Jb. xxvii. 3), and Elihu, the last of Job's tormentors, says: 'The spirit of God hath made me, and the breath of the Almighty giveth me life' (Jb. xxxiii. 4). The general principle involved is put by the Psalmist this way: 'Thou takest away their breath, they die, and return to their dust. Thou sendest forth thy spirit, they are created' (Ps. civ. 29f.).

It is more than difficult to be absolutely sure when *ruach* denotes 'breath' and when it signifies 'spirit'. But what is not in doubt is that, either way, the men of the Old Testament consistently looked to the Lord as the source of all life. When He gives His Spirit men live, and when He does not they die. It is as simple as that. It is only as and where the Spirit of the Lord is that there is life.

THE SPIRIT AMONG MEN

The work of the Spirit, of course, does not cease when men are given life. He continues vigorously at work among them. Interesting and varied results ensue.

If we may begin on the lowest level, it was widely held among the people of antiquity that a madman, a man who does not act according to the rational ways of mankind, is indwelt by some minor god or spirit. From that it was but a step to the idea that whenever a man was very close to his god he would not behave in a manner predictable by men in general. Thus in many religions the sign that a man was a prophet was that he would go off into an ecstasy, accompanied by physical movements of various kinds. It was only when the frenzy was upon him that he would be so very different from the ordinary run of mankind. Only then would he give a word from another world. Even such a thinker as Plato speaks of connecting 'the very word mania with the noblest of arts, that which foretells the future, by calling it the manic art'.[1] He thinks that 'the prophetess at Delphi and the

---

[1] *Phaedrus*, 244 C (Loeb edition).

priestesses at Dodona when they have been mad have con-
ferred many splendid benefits upon Greece both in private
and in public affairs, but few or none when they have been
in their right minds'.[1]

This kind of exterior commendation of their message was
not the characteristic of the prophets of Israel. They were
quite different. Nevertheless it was held in Israel that when the
Spirit came upon a man he might behave in a way not so
very different from the frenzied prophet of the ancient
Middle East in general (cf. Ho. ix. 7, 'the prophet is a fool, the
man that hath the spirit is mad'). This happened to Saul the
king. On one occasion he was 'turned into another man'
(1 Sa. x. 6). On another he 'stripped off his clothes, and he also
prophesied before Samuel, and lay down naked all that day
and all that night' (1 Sa. xix. 24). This is not what we, with
our more sophisticated approach, would have anticipated.
But there is no predicting what will happen when the Spirit
comes upon a man. It is abundantly clear that the people who
observed Saul on both occasions were impressed.

A variety of physical endowments is due to the indwelling
Spirit. A very well-known example is the great strength of
Samson. The initial manifestation of his potentialities, evidently a kind of foretaste of things to come, is due to the
Spirit (Jdg. xiii. 25). Then when his first deed of strength is
recorded, the slaying of a lion with his bare hands, this is
prefixed by the assertion, 'the spirit of the Lord came mightily
upon him' (Jdg. xiv. 6). It is the same thing with his slaying
of the Philistines after the wedding guests had guessed his
riddle (Jdg. xiv. 19), and with his breaking of the ropes that

---

[1] *Op. cit.*, 244 B. Similarly Plato explains the origin of poetry in
terms of a madness akin to prophecy: 'For a poet is a light and winged
and sacred thing, and is unable ever to indite until he has been inspired
and put out of his senses and his mind is no longer in him. . . . And for
this reason God takes away the mind of these men and uses them as his
ministers, just as he does soothsayers and godly seers, in order that we
who hear them may know that it is not they who utter these words of
great price, when they are out of their wits, but that it is God himself
who speaks and addresses us through them' (*Ion*, 534 B, C; Loeb
edition).

bound him (Jdg. xv. 14). Throughout the Samson stories it is accepted that the young hero's strength is not due to anything inherent in him, but to the presence of the Spirit of the Lord. When the Lord departed from him (Jdg. xvi. 20), so did his strength.

The Spirit not only gave strength; He gave skill. Thus the Lord called Bezalel, the craftsman, and 'filled him with the spirit of God, in wisdom, and in understanding, and in knowledge, and in all manner of workmanship, to devise cunning works, to work in gold, and in silver, and in brass, and in cutting of stones for setting, and in carving of wood, to work in all manner of workmanship' (Ex. xxxi. 3–5). We sometimes talk about a musician, or a painter, as 'inspired'. The Hebrews did the same thing with regard to Bezalel, but they took it literally. The tabernacle was to be a place made to the divine plan. It was to be worthy of worship of so great a God. Therefore the man who was to superintend all its fine workmanship must be filled with the Spirit of God. The same must be said about those who prepared the high priest's glorious robes (Ex. xxviii. 3). This gives rise to the rather daring conjecture (daring for men of antiquity, that is) that these may have been women, for women were engaged on somewhat similar work in 2 Kings xxiii. 7.

The Spirit gives wisdom in a more general sense than the specialized knowledge of the craftsman. The judges who delivered Israel from time to time are said to do so under the leadership of the Spirit. Thus the Spirit of the Lord 'came upon' Othniel (Jdg. iii. 10) and Jephthah (Jdg. xi. 29), while in a very vivid expression the narrator tells us that the Spirit 'clothed Himself with' Gideon (see Jdg. vi. 34). Of this latter piece of imagery Burney can say, 'The meaning seems to be that the divine spirit took complete possession of Gideon, so that he became, as it were, its incarnation, and was thus employed as its instrument'.[1] The whole narrative makes it clear that the judges did not accomplish their great deeds of deliverance because of any natural strength, leadership, or

---

[1] *The Book of Judges*, London, 1939, *in loc.*

wisdom that they possessed. Each is God's chosen man for the particular hour. God has given him the gifts he needs to carry out the work of deliverance. In other words he is a judge only because God has put His Spirit within him. Similarly Joseph was 'a man in whom the spirit of God is' (Gn. xli. 38), Joshua was 'full of the spirit of wisdom' (Dt. xxxiv. 9), David was equipped to be king in that 'the spirit of the Lord came mightily upon' him (1 Sa. xvi. 13). Nehemiah records a prayer which ascribes the knowledge of the Israelites in the wilderness to God's Spirit. 'Thou gavest also thy good spirit to instruct them' (Ne. ix. 20). The great thought behind all these passages is that a man may become the vehicle of God's purposes. With the Spirit of God within him, he may play his part in setting forth the divine purpose. This gives dignity to the whole of life. It gives meaning to life.

We have already noticed that a prophetic frenzy came upon Saul the king, causing men to ask 'Is Saul also among the prophets?' (1 Sa. x. 12, xix. 24). What is much more significant is that the Spirit of God gave their message to the great prophets of Israel. Ezekiel tells us that on a certain occasion 'the spirit of the Lord fell upon me, and he said unto me, Speak, Thus saith the Lord' (Ezk. xi. 5). Then (and only then) came the prophet's message. Ezekiel uses similar expressions elsewhere (Ezk. ii. 2, iii. 24, etc.). The message of Balaam apparently came the same way (Nu. xxiv. 2). So did that of Amasai (1 Ch. xii. 18). So did that of Zechariah the son of Jehoiada (2 Ch. xxiv. 20).[1] The total message of the pre-exilic prophets is ascribed to the Spirit (Ne. ix. 30; Zc. vii. 12). The message of the prophet follows the statement that 'the spirit of the Lord God is upon me' in Isaiah lxi. 1. Micah is 'full of power' to declare his message 'by the spirit of the Lord' (Mi. iii. 8). It is a consistent strand of Old Testament teaching that the Lord gives the prophets His message through His Spirit. Their inspired words are not the fruits of their brooding over the situation and then giving their verdict.

[1] In the last two mentioned. Amasai and Zechariah, we have the same vivid metaphor as with Gideon, that the Spirit 'clothed Himself with' them.

They are the product of a divine activity. They result from the work of the Spirit of God within the servants of God.[1]

THE ETHICAL NOTE

When we consider the way contemporary thought emphasizes ecstatic ravings and the like, perhaps the most surprising as well as significant part of Old Testament thought on the Spirit is that which stresses the ethical note. As we have seen, there are not wanting passages which see the presence of the Spirit in ecstasies of various kinds. But the more distinctive teaching of the Old Testament is that the Spirit gives ethical perception and power to live well.

The prophet Micah in a notable passage attributes his ability to denounce evil to the presence of the Spirit. 'I truly am full of power by the spirit of the Lord, and of judgement, and of might, to declare unto Jacob his transgression, and to Israel his sin' (Mi. iii. 8). The prophet might thunder out his denunciations of evil. Indeed, as everyone knew, that was the characteristic thing about the true prophets of the Lord. They were always doing it. But the point that Micah makes is that the prophet does not do this because he is a superbly wise man, or because he is a superbly virtuous man, or because he is a supremely self-important man. He does it because the Spirit of the Lord is within him. The Spirit gives him the insight to know with crystal clarity what are the things he should denounce, and the Spirit gives him the courage and burning zeal which cannot rest.

Jeremiah, like other prophets, underwent difficult experiences in proclaiming his message. Sometimes, he tells us, he was tempted not to speak of the Lord. But 'then there is

[1] We might have expected that there would be a more frequent ascription of the message of the prophets to the Spirit. Their reserve in the use of the term 'Spirit' is probably due to the associations the term had aroused from its use by the ecstatic prophets of other religions. The prophets of Israel did not wish to be classed with such men. Yet the passages we have cited are sufficient to show that, though they might not say so very often, the prophets did believe that their message came through the Spirit of the Lord.

in mine heart as it were a burning fire shut up in my bones, and I am weary with forbearing, and I cannot contain' (Je. xx. 9). He does not mention the Spirit explicitly, but his experience is not unlike that outlined by Micah. It is the Spirit within that enables, yea, compels the prophet to utter his condemnations of evil and his urgings to good.

Nor is such a manifestation of the Spirit confined to the great prophets. In its way it is granted to ordinary men and with somewhat similar results. Thus we find the Psalmist praying, 'Teach me to do thy will; for thou art my God: thy spirit is good; lead me in the land of uprightness' (Ps. cxliii. 10). He longed to do the will of God. He wanted to walk in the way of uprightness. So he looked to the Spirit of God, that good Spirit, 'which willingly furthers the salvation of man'.[1] Similarly, the prayer, 'Cast me not away from thy presence; and take not thy holy spirit from me' (Ps. li. 11), expresses the desire to walk in the ways of God and to do the will of God. As A. B. Davidson says, it 'is almost equal to a prayer that his mind may not cease to be religious, to have thoughts of God, and aspirations towards God'.[2]

The spirit is good (Ne. ix. 20). The Spirit is poured upon men 'from on high' (Is. xxxii. 15). Specific examples of men to whom this happened include Moses and the elders (Nu. xi. 17, 25), Joshua (Nu. xxvii. 18), the Servant of the Lord (Is. xlii. 1), the Servant's seed (=Israel? Is. xliv. 3), and 'them that turn from transgression in Jacob' (Is. lix. 20f.). Negatively, sinners may be described as rebelling and as grieving God's holy Spirit (Is. lxiii. 10).

In many places we find the thought that good works of one kind and another are due to the Spirit. Notably is this so in the renewal of the whole man for which Ezekiel looks. A piece of moral patchwork is not sufficient. So the prophet speaks of the day when the Lord will cleanse the people from all their iniquity. God will give men a new heart and a new spirit. God says, 'And I will put my spirit within you, and cause you to walk in my statutes, and ye shall keep my

[1] F. Delitzsch, in loc.
[2] The Theology of the Old Testament, Edinburgh, 1904, p. 124.

judgements, and do them' (Ezk. xxxvi. 27). There could be no more emphatic way of saying that men cannot reach God's standard in their own strength, and that they need the very life of God within them if they are to be the sort of people that God would have them be. It is possibly something of the sort that Zechariah has in mind when he says that the Lord will 'pour upon the house of David, and upon the inhabitants of Jerusalem, the spirit of grace and of supplication' (Zc. xii. 10).

In all this we have come a long way from the idea of the heathen, that the Spirit is to be discerned in frenzied ecstasies. Without yielding for one moment the thought that the Spirit may take men in unusual fashion, the men of the Old Testament discerned that the heart of the matter was not there. What was more profound and more significant was the thought that the Spirit could and would change men's outlook. For the most part they looked on this as a future prospect. But they were sure that one day the Spirit would come upon them with all the power of God and make them into the sort of people that they ought to be.

A FUTURE OUTPOURING

Manifold and striking though the present work of the Spirit was in the judgment of the Old Testament writers, the best was yet to be. They recognized that what they saw of the Spirit of God was far from exhausting the possibilities. They looked and longed for a day when God would intervene in the affairs of men with striking results. And sometimes they interpreted the great day in terms of the activity of the Spirit.

Moses once expressed the desire that 'all the Lord's people were prophets, that the Lord would put his spirit upon them!' (Nu. xi. 29). Isaiah and Ezekiel look forward to a work of the Spirit among men (Is. xliv. 3; Ezk. xxxvi. 26f.). But probably the classical passage is to be found in the little prophecy of Joel. The time of this prophecy is uncertain, but it was not long after a disastrous plague of locusts which Joel saw as the judgment of God. He used this as his text for calling upon the people to repent of all their sins and to turn to their God, 'for he is gracious and full of compassion, slow to anger, and plenteous in mercy' (Joel ii. 13). Then he looked through all the troubles of the present time to the latter days of which the Lord says, 'I will pour out my spirit upon all flesh . . . and also upon the servants and upon the handmaids in those days will I pour out my spirit' (Joel ii. 28f.). All are included, men and women, bond and free. This will be an activity of the Spirit, the like of which men have never before seen.

We have already noticed that Ezekiel looks for the day when God will put a new heart and a new spirit within His people. This, too, is for him a future activity, an occasion when the Lord will do a mighty work, the like of which the prophet has not hitherto seen. Isaiah adds the point that the great work of the Spirit will be associated with 'a shoot out of the stock of Jesse, and a branch out of his roots'. He goes on, 'the spirit of the Lord shall rest upon him, the spirit of wisdom and understanding, the spirit of counsel and might, the spirit of knowledge and of the fear of the Lord' (Is. xi. 1–3). That the prophet does not conceive of the work of the Spirit as ended when the Messiah is equipped is clear from the following passage, which goes on to speak of the transformation of all things. From Isaiah lix. 21 we learn that the future gift of the Spirit is not transitory, but 'for ever'.

The Old Testament, then, ascribes a multiplicity of activities among men to the work of the Spirit. But it does not think of anything present as manifesting the full revelation of this Spirit. It points us forward to a coming day, a day when the Messiah should appear, a day when the Spirit should be poured out upon all (and not restricted to any one class of people, like prophets), a day when men should know complete renewal of their inner life by the divine power that should be given to them.

THE SPIRIT AND GOD

Christians read the Old Testament in the light of the New. From the later revelation we have come to think of the nature of God as Triune, so that within the Godhead we find God the Father, God the Son, and God the Holy Spirit. It must be recognized that this is a New Testament revelation, and that with no more than the Old Testament in our hands we should never have risen to this knowledge of God. Nevertheless it is inevitable that Christian people should ask how far the New Testament doctrine of the Spirit is foreshadowed in the Old.

We have seen that the Old Testament consistently links the Spirit with God. What the Spirit does is the work of God. That, I think, is not in dispute. But we may well go on to ask whether the Spirit is thought of as in any way distinct from God the Father, or whether He is no more than another name for the Father (as in the case of a man's own spirit), or perhaps for an aspect of the Father (as God in action). Here it must be confessed that there is nothing that compels us to regard the Spirit in a Trinitarian fashion. It is enough to give us cause for praise that devout and learned Jews, making a very close study of the Old Testament with a reverent acceptance of what it says as the very Word of God, yet do not come to a belief in a Spirit in any way separate from the Father. The Spirit as distinct from the Father is a New Testament doctrine.

Yet there are passages which, at the very least, give us hints in this direction. Thus in Isaiah xlviii. 16 we read: 'now the Lord God hath sent me, and his spirit.' It may be that the Spirit is in no sense distinct from the Lord God in this passage, but to say the least the words lend themselves to interpretation in a different sense. Other passages are easier to interpret on the supposition that the Spirit in question is the same as the Father, but they at least awake our question. Such are 'they rebelled, and grieved his holy spirit' (Is. lxiii. 10); 'where is he that put his holy spirit in the midst of them?' (Is. lxiii. 11); 'my spirit abode among you' (Hg. ii. 5); 'Not by might, nor by power, but by my spirit, saith the Lord of hosts' (Zc. iv. 6). There are others, but these are typical. They do not demonstrate a Trinitarian view. But they show that there are Old Testament passages which indicate more than a bare unitarianism. They gain in force when they are understood in the light of the clearer New Testament teaching. And in turn New

Testament teaching is illuminated when we allow Old Testament teaching on the Spirit to shine upon it.

We conclude this section with some words of C. Ryder Smith. Speaking of terms like 'spirit', 'wisdom', 'word', and 'the glory', he says: 'With all of these it is impossible to say whether they are one with God or separate from Him. To use an old comparison, they are as much one with Him and as much separate as the sunshine is one with the sun and separate from it. They say at one and the same time that the God is awe-fully separate from man and yet that He comes near to him. A Christian would say that they show the need for the Incarnation.'[1]

[1] *The Religion of the Hebrews*, London, 1935, p. 127.

CHAPTER III

A PERSON OR A THING?

FROM the foregoing it is clear that our understanding of the Holy Spirit must be primarily derived from the New Testament. While the Old Testament has much that we can gratefully receive, the really distinctive teaching on the Spirit comes from the New. In John vii. 39 we read that 'the Spirit was not yet given; because Jesus was not yet glorified'. The meaning of these words is not exactly obvious. But this, at least, is plain: the Spirit had never up to that time been given in the fullest sense, nor would the Spirit be given until Jesus was glorified.[1] In other words, the Spirit, in the New Testament understanding of it all, is given to men as a result of the work of Jesus Christ.

The New Testament keeps on stressing the intimate connection between the Spirit and Jesus. They are linked in the closest possible fashion. The Spirit is 'the Spirit of Jesus' (Acts xvi. 7), 'the Spirit of Jesus Christ' (Phil. i. 19), 'the Spirit of Christ' (Rom. viii. 9), 'the Spirit of his Son' (Gal. iv. 6). The work of Christ and the work of the Spirit are

[1] This may give us part of the reason for the rather strange fact, to which C. K. Barrett has drawn attention so forcefully (*The Holy Spirit and the Gospel Tradition*, London, 1947), that in the Synoptic Gospels Jesus very rarely speaks of the Spirit. Part of the explanation may be, as Newton Flew thinks, that the word 'Spirit' had been so debased by ecstatics claiming to be spirit-possessed that it was necessary that a fuller and better idea be lived out in Jesus' ministry, before it could be taught. Again, the way to Pentecost is via Calvary, and the disciples understood so little of the latter that our Lord may well have felt there was no point in giving full instruction about the former But, though we may conjecture, we really do not know. W. F. Lofthouse reminds us that 'The source of the conception of the Spirit in Ac 1-15 must be found in the teaching of Jesus. We can look for it nowhere else' (*The Expository Times*, vol. LII, p. 336). This, he suggests, points to the historicity of John's Gospel, in speaking of teaching on the Spirit during the farewell discourses.

inextricably intertwined. The Spirit is to bear witness of
Jesus (Jn. xv. 26), to remind people of what Jesus had said
(Jn. xiv. 26), to glorify Jesus (Jn. xvi. 14).

There can be no denying that the New Testament is marked
by a great outburst of the Spirit's activity. Because of this
some have suggested that 'The Acts of the Apostles' would be
better named 'The Acts of the Holy Spirit'. As Giuseppe
Ricciotti has said, 'The Gospels are the story of those things
which Christ did and said, while the Acts are the story of those
things which the other Paraclete did and said.'[1] And this great
outburst of activity is always regarded as one of the consequences of the incarnation.[2] 'There is no reference in the New
Testament to any work of the Spirit apart from Christ. The
Spirit is, in an exclusive sense, the Spirit of Christ'.[3]

H. J. Wotherspoon lays stress on this connection with
Christ. The Spirit 'reaches us through the Lord Jesus, as the
light shines into the Temple through the pictured glass, the
same light that pours from the sun, but coloured by the
medium through which it passes, and carrying to the wall on
which it now falls the image of the figure through which it
shines. So the Holy Spirit reaches us, tinged as it were, by the
nature through which He is mediated to us, undistinguishable
in character from the soul of the Lord Himself, bearing to us
His thoughts, His emotions, His impulses, impressing upon
us His will, permeating our being with His vitality'.[4]

It is important to be clear on this, more especially in view
of some who talk of a 'dispensation of the Spirit' in such a

---

[1] Cited in *The Expository Times*, vol. LXX, p. 13.

[2] Cf. H. Wheeler Robinson, 'Within the period covered by the New
Testament the new fact of history—Jesus Christ—created a new order
of experience of the Holy Spirit, viz. a personal relation to God
through Christ' (*The Christian Experience of the Holy Spirit*, London,
1947, p. 132).

[3] George S. Hendry, *The Holy Spirit in Christian Theology*, London,
1957, p. 26. So important is this to Prof. Hendry that he begins his book,
not with the Old Testament, but with a chapter entitled 'The Holy
Spirit and Christ'. The Holy Spirit cannot be understood apart from
His connection with Christ.

[4] *What Happened at Pentecost?*, Edinburgh, 1937, p. 36.

way as to imply that Pentecost has made possible a relationship to God independent of Christ. It can never be stressed too strongly that the Christian is what he is because of what Christ has done. The work of the Spirit is never in competition with or in opposition to the work of Christ. The Spirit is 'the Spirit of Christ'. Their work is a harmonious blend. Indeed it is one. S. D. Gordon in his inimitable fashion puts it this way: 'The Lord Jesus draws a cheque for my use. The Spirit cashes that cheque and puts the money into my hands. Jesus does in me now by His Spirit what He did for me centuries ago on the cross, in His person.'[1]

Consequently, for the rest of this book, we will be taken up with the New Testament revelation of the Spirit. We will not be able to deal at all fully with what is a vast mass of evidence. But we will select certain aspects of New Testament teaching which seem to be important, and try to find their relevance to men of today.

First we face questions like: Is the Spirit a Person or a thing? Is the Spirit a real live Being like the Father or the Son? Or a power, an influence, a force effecting the divine purpose? Most people refer to the Spirit as 'It'. Are they right? Or should we talk about the Spirit in personal terms, 'He' and 'Him'?

Now the main thrust of New Testament teaching is plain enough. There the Spirit is consistently regarded as a Person. The ordinary usage I imagine rises from the sheer difficulty of thinking of the Spirit as a Person. Most people have a very nebulous idea of the Spirit. For them the Spirit is a means of strength to the Christian, a divine power. But the Spirit has no form that can be seen, no voice that can be heard, and we do tend to associate personality with a being in bodily form. The Spirit is unlike any person that we know, and there's the rub. Because He is so different we find it difficult to hold a clear-cut conception about Him. And since our idea of the Spirit is hazy we tend insensibly to think and speak about Him in impersonal terms.

[1] *Quiet Talks on Power*, London, n.d., p. 64.

There does not seem to be much difficulty in thinking of God the Father as personal. The very idea implicit in the word 'Father' ensures that we regard Him as a Person in the very fullest sense of that term. We habitually address prayer to Him. We rest in the assurance that He watches over us. We know that He loves us. Always we think of Him in personal terms. We would not dream of calling Him 'It'.

If anything, it is even easier to think of the Son in a personal way. He is the Babe of Bethlehem, the Carpenter of Nazareth, the Teacher of Galilee. The facts of His life, known to us so vividly from the Gospels, forbid us to think of Him in any other way. And although we realize that the ascension means certain changes in our understanding of His Being, we do not for one moment cease to think of Him as a Person.

But it is different with the Spirit. 'Spirit' is not such an aggressively personal word as 'Father'. The Spirit has not become incarnate like the Son. We find it hard to picture Him. His workings are for the most part inward and secret, we might almost say mystical. He gives us grace, guidance, strength and the like, which we might easily ascribe to a force or influence proceeding from the Father. In the English language, as also in Greek, 'Spirit' is a neuter noun, and we find it easier to think of neuters as things than as people. When the New Testament writers want to speak of the Spirit the symbols they use, oil, fire and the like, are usually such as might readily be interpreted of an inanimate force or influence.

All this means that, if we are to think of the Spirit in any other way than as a thing, it will need a special effort on our part to listen to the evidence. We are naturally predisposed to refer to Him and to think of Him as a power emanating from on high, to think of Him as 'It'. But in a matter as important as this we must not be guided by our presuppositions. It is imperative that we be guided by the evidence.

THE PARACLETE

Let us begin by noticing some of the ways in which the Spirit is described. First He is spoken of as 'the Comforter'

(Jn. xiv. 16, 26, xv. 26, xvi. 7). This is a rather misleading translation of the Greek word *paraklētos*. Elsewhere in the New Testament it is found only in 1 John ii. 1, where it is used of Jesus Christ, and is translated 'Advocate': 'And if any man sin, we have an Advocate with the Father, Jesus Christ the righteous.' This passage reflects the essentially legal meaning of the term. Etymologically *paraklētos* means 'one called to the side of' another. But calling someone alongside is always for the purpose of receiving help, and thus the one who responds to the call is one who is committed to giving assistance. The word came to be used particularly in legal matters, where it denoted 'the counsel for the defence'. Hence the translation 'Advocate' in 1 John. But this has to be understood in a wider sense than with us. When a man in ancient Greece was in legal trouble, he tended to gather all the helpers he could. They need not necessarily be legal people. If they could only come and say, 'I wasn't there at the time, and didn't see what happened, but I know my friend would not have done this!' they might be called paracletes.[1]

The point of importance for us is that the word was applied to persons. However we translate it (and something like 'Helper' might be the meaning in the Johannine passage), in the first century it would be understood of a person. Certainly nobody then would have imagined that the word would denote a vague influence, a power flowing from God. Its use marks the Spirit as a Person.

So does the way the Spirit is spoken of in general throughout these chapters. Here we must draw attention to a point of Greek grammar which is not obvious in our English translation. Indeed it is not possible to bring it out at all, because English (alone, so I am told, among the important languages of either ancient or modern times) has escaped the phenomenon of grammatical gender. With us gender is a simple

---

[1] Moulton and Milligan quote Field as giving the meaning, 'a friend of the accused person, called to speak to his character, or otherwise enlist the sympathy of the judges' (*The Vocabulary of the Greek Testament*, London, 1926, *sub voce*).

affair. Nouns referring to the masculine sex are masculine, to the feminine sex are feminine. All the rest are neuter. It is beautifully simple. But it is not so in other languages. In Latin, for example, a table is feminine, and we must call it 'she'. In German a maiden is neuter and should be called 'it'. In French a hat is masculine and must be referred to as 'he'. It is all very confusing.

Now in Greek the word for 'Spirit' is neuter, and should in strict grammar be referred to as 'It'. When John uses a pronoun to refer to 'Spirit' and the two words are close together, he usually respects his grammar and uses the correct form 'It'. But if a word or two intervenes he nearly always uses the masculine form 'He'. This is grammatically incorrect, but most illuminating. The explanation is surely that John habitually thought of the Spirit in personal terms, as 'He' rather than as 'It'. Naturally enough his thinking dictated this form of speech. Where he can, he uses personal forms of the pronouns. He even does it occasionally where the pronoun and the word for Spirit occur side by side. See John xvi. 13, 'he, the Spirit of truth'.

While we are on these more or less abstruse points of Greek grammar we might add another. In Greek there are two words for 'other': *allos* means 'another of the same kind', while *heteros* points rather to 'another of a different kind'. Thus if I ask for another book, using *allos*, I am seeking another copy of the volume in question. But if you bring me a copy of another book altogether I might complain that I didn't say *heteros*. When Jesus speaks of the Spirit as 'another Comforter' (Jn. xiv. 16) the word He uses is *allos*. The most natural interpretation of all this is that the Spirit is to be thought of as another like Jesus. As Jesus is a Person, the inference is that the Spirit is also a Person. The only catch in the reasoning is that not all Greek writers used the two words for 'other' strictly. Some did; some did not. It is not completely certain that John did (he uses *heteros* so rarely that we cannot be sure). But as far as it goes the point is valid. The most natural way of understanding 'another' is 'another of like kind'.

This accords with what we read in John's Gospel generally concerning the Spirit. There are references to the Spirit in the story of Nicodemus (Jn. iii). The Spirit could not be given till Jesus was glorified (Jn. vii. 39). Jesus bestowed the Spirit on the disciples (Jn. xx. 22). But the really significant teaching on this subject comes in five passages in the farewell discourse, namely, John xiv. 15–17, 25f., xv. 26f., xvi. 5–11 and 12–15. If we look up these verses we will see that the Spirit is always spoken of as though He were a Person. He will remind men of what Jesus had said (Jn. xiv. 26), He will teach them (*ibid.*), He will 'bear witness' of Jesus (Jn. xv. 26), He will guide men (Jn. xvi. 13), He hears and speaks (*ibid.*), He will glorify Jesus (Jn. xvi. 14), He will 'declare' certain things (*ibid.*).

One or two of these expressions might conceivably be accidental or metaphorical. But the combined weight of them all is impressive. It is clear that in John's Gospel the Spirit is thought of consistently as a Person, and not simply as an influence or power.

THE SPIRIT IN PAULINE WRITINGS

For Paul, the Spirit occupies a very large place indeed. He can go so far as to say 'if any man hath not the Spirit of Christ, he is none of his' (Rom. viii. 9), and positively, 'as many as are led by the Spirit of God, these are sons of God' (Rom. viii. 14). It is recorded in Acts that when on one occasion he met certain men who claimed to be Christians, the first question he asked was 'Did ye receive the Holy Ghost when ye believed?' (Acts xix. 2). Doubtless he was considerably shocked when they replied, 'Nay, we did not so much as hear whether the Holy Ghost was given' (*ibid.*). He took immediate steps to rectify the position.

In accordance with his view that the Spirit occupies such an important place in the Christian scheme of things, Paul's Epistles abound in references to the Spirit. Unfortunately for our purpose he never seems to have tried to answer the kind of question that we persist in asking. In particular, Paul never deals systematically with the personality of the Spirit. He never says in so many words, 'The Spirit is a Person'. However, if we hunt through his references to the Spirit we will, I think, be left in no doubt but that he, like John, thought of the Spirit in personal terms.

Paul's usual method is to speak of the Spirit as active in some way. But from the activities that he attributes to the Spirit, we can see that the Spirit must be a Person. Take for example 1 Corinthians xii. 11: 'but all these worketh the one and the same Spirit, dividing to each one severally even as he will.' It is not impossible, I suppose, to hold that Paul would have thought of an impersonal agency as 'working'. But it is much more likely that he ascribes work to a person. And still more must this be said of the reference to the will. 'Even as he will' has no meaning with reference to inanimate objects. Will is the characteristic activity of personal life. It must refer to a person.

This kind of thinking characterizes Paul's approach to the Spirit. He can refer to 'the mind of the Spirit' (Rom. viii. 27), which envisages the Spirit as a thinking entity. So does the reference to the things that the Spirit 'knoweth' (1 Cor. ii. 11). But the Spirit is not a coldly intellectual Being. Paul speaks of 'the love of the Spirit' (Rom. xv. 30), and he can think of the Spirit as being grieved (Eph. iv. 30). The Spirit's love and care for men is seen in the fact of His intercession for them (it is 'with groanings which cannot be uttered', Rom. viii. 26, which points to intensity, and it is 'according to the will of God', Rom. viii. 27, which emphasizes His unity with the Father). Paul uses bold imagery in informing us that the Spirit 'cries out' (Gal. iv. 6). The Spirit dwells in men (Rom. viii. 9). The Spirit leads men (Rom. viii. 14). The Spirit bears witness with the spirit of men (Rom. viii. 16). The Spirit teaches men (1 Cor. ii. 13).

All this is not the systematic exposition of doctrine. Paul is not trying to unfold all the implications of the Christian view of the Spirit. He is dealing with the problems that arose during the course of a busy practical ministry. He is writing to churches and to individuals about specific needs, and mentioning, as he deals with those needs, certain facets of the

Spirit's activities. These incidental glimpses of the apostle's thinking are all the more revealing. They show us that Paul habitually thought of the Spirit as a Person. The terms that he naturally uses to describe what the Spirit does are terms that we just as naturally employ to describe what people do.

It is in keeping with this that he repeatedly joins the Spirit with the Father and the Son. For example: 'The grace of the Lord Jesus Christ, and the love of God, and the communion of the Holy Ghost, be with you all' (2 Cor. xiii. 14; cf. also 1 Cor. xii. 4–6; Eph. iv. 4–6, etc.). It is inconceivable that in such threefold passages Paul means us to understand that the Father and the Son are Persons, but the Spirit is not. The use of the three in the Pauline manner is a strong indication that Paul conceived of the Spirit as just as fully personal as the other two.

DISTINCT FROM THE FATHER AND THE SON

That brings us to the question of the relation between the Spirit on the one hand and the Father and the Son on the other. If it be granted that the references to the Spirit show Him to be personal, it may be retorted that this is natural enough for the reason that the Spirit is simply another name for one or other of these. The Spirit may be thought of as the *alter ego* of the Father, or alternatively, of the Son. If this were the case, it would be no matter for surprise that He proves to be personal. But it would mean a very different view of the Godhead.

Most of the New Testament references to the Spirit refer to Him as at work in one way or another, but without any reference to either the Father or the Son. To select an example at random: 'to one is given through the Spirit the word of wisdom' (1 Cor. xii. 8). Here we see the Spirit doing something within a believer. It is not absolutely impossible to see in this an activity of the Father or of the Son, but that is not what one would expect from a simple reading of the text. There it appears that the Spirit is a Being in His own right.

The same could be said of very many New Testament passages. This does not amount to proof, but the cumulative force of many instances is impressive.

But we are not left to inferences of this kind, weighty though we may hold them to be. There are passages which speak of all three Persons of the Trinity together. Such are 'the grace' of 2 Corinthians xiii. 14, the 'unities' of Ephesians iv. 4-6, and the 'diversities' of 1 Corinthians xii. 4-6. Such, too, is the baptismal formula of Matthew xxviii. 19. Such, too, is Mark i. 10f., where we read of the Spirit coming upon the Son in form like a dove, while the voice of the Father is heard from heaven. Each of the Three has a part in this incident, and none of them can be identical with either of the other two.

In similar fashion we find the Son praying to the Father that He will send the Spirit (Jn. xiv. 16). Indeed, both Father and Son are commonly concerned in the mission of the Spirit (Jn. xiv. 26, xv. 26, xvi. 15). Sometimes all Three are referred to together in other connections, as when we read 'through him (i.e. Christ) we both have our access in one Spirit unto the Father' (Eph. ii. 18), or, for a double mention of all Three, 'But if the Spirit of him that raised up Jesus from the dead dwelleth in you, he that raised up Christ Jesus from the dead shall quicken also your mortal bodies through his Spirit that dwelleth in you' (Rom. viii. 11). (See also Rom. xv. 16; 1 Cor. vi. 11; 2 Thes. ii. 13; Tit. iii. 4-6; 1 Pet. i. 2; Jude 20f.) This group of passages is sufficiently large for us to see that it is a New Testament habit to think of the three Persons together. But to group them in this fashion is to regard them as co-ordinate with and distinct from each other.

There are some passages which refer to two of the Three in such a way as to make it difficult to think of them as identical. For example, in John xvi. 7, Jesus tells us that 'It is expedient for you that I go away: for if I go not away, the Comforter will not come unto you; but if I go, I will send him unto you'. It is very difficult indeed to see how this could take place if Jesus and the Spirit were thought of as identical. Again, in Romans viii. 26f., the Spirit is pictured as making intercession for us, i.e. intercession to the Father. Which seems to rule out the possibility that He is identical with the Father.

It seems clear, then, that the New Testament, while speaking a great deal about the Spirit, and while associating Him in the closest possible fashion with the Father and the Son, yet keeps the Three in some sense distinct. In particular, it does not teach that the Spirit is to be equated with either of the others.

OBJECTIONS

Occasionally it is objected that all this depends on a selection of passages. Other passages, it is said, tell a different story. When we ask 'Which others?' they appear to be chiefly certain parts of the farewell discourse in John's Gospel, and two passages in Paul's Corinthian correspondence.

The Johannine passages are as follows: 'I will not leave you desolate: I come unto you' (xiv. 18); 'A little while, and ye behold me no more; and again a little while, and ye shall see me' (xvi. 16); 'he breathed on them, and saith unto them, Receive ye the Holy Ghost' (xx. 22). The first two are urged to mean that Jesus is about to leave the disciples, but that in the coming of the Spirit He will return to them. Therefore He must be thought of as identical with the Spirit. To this it must be rejoined in the first place that the passages do not necessarily point to the coming of the Spirit. They are perfectly capable of being understood in terms of the resurrection appearances, and, indeed, not a few students take them so. Moreover, even if it be conceded that they refer to the Spirit's coming, that would not argue an identity. Jesus speaks of the Spirit as sent by Himself (xvi. 7). He carries on the work of Jesus (xvi. 13f.). Under these circumstances it might well be said that Jesus comes in the Spirit's coming without that meaning that the distinction between the two is obliterated.

The third Johannine passage is interpreted in the objection as meaning that Jesus was imparting to the disciples the blessing of His own holy presence with them. This is not easy to maintain. In the Johannine narrative Jesus is standing there

in the midst of the apostles both before and after the incident
of the breathing. Whatever He imparted to them, He Himself
appears to remain distinct from it. It is really more than difficult to think of Jesus as giving them Himself. The Spirit of
which He speaks is clearly other than He.

One of the Pauline passages is 1 Corinthians xv. 45: 'The
ast Adam became a life-giving spirit.' There is no question
but that 'the last Adam' refers to Christ, but it is otherwise
with the contention that 'a life-giving spirit' means 'the Holy
Spirit' of whom we read elsewhere. It no more equates Jesus
with the Holy Spirit than the statement 'God is a Spirit'
(Jn. iv. 24) equates Him with the Father. The passage simply
affirms that Jesus is a spirit and that He gives life.

The other passage is 2 Corinthians iii. 17f.: 'Now the Lord
is the Spirit: and where the Spirit of the Lord is, there is
liberty. . . . But we all . . . are transformed into the same image
from glory to glory, even as from the Lord the Spirit.' This,
it is alleged, simply equates the Lord and the Spirit. But it is
not so simple. The passage may well be understood by denying that 'the Spirit' means 'the Holy Spirit'. In the context
Paul is contrasting 'the ministration of death' (verse 7) with
'the ministration of the spirit' (verse 8). It is thus natural
enough to speak of the Lord Jesus as 'the Spirit' who brings
in the new covenant. This evokes the thought of 'the Spirit
of the Lord' and Paul makes the transition. But this does not
mean that the Spirit and the Lord are one in any other sense
than that in which the Father and the Son are one (Jn. x. 30).[1]
Paul is not giving a theoretical description of the nature of
the Lord (or of the Spirit). He is affirming in strong terms that
He is the source of spiritual life, and that in this He works in
the closest association with the Spirit. In any case it is to be
noted that immediately after speaking of the Lord as the

---

[1] Cf. R. V. G. Tasker, 'Paul is not here confounding the Persons of
the Trinity by identifying Christ and the Spirit, but showing that
because of the Holy Spirit the influence of Christ is universal in its
effect and unlimited in its power. The Lord and the Spirit are "one" in
the same sense that Jesus said that He and the Father were one' (*Tyndale
Commentary* on 2 Cor. iii. 17).

Spirit Paul goes on to refer to 'the Spirit of the Lord'. He at once distinguishes between them.

Alternatively we may understand 'the Spirit' to mean 'the Holy Spirit', but this will not signify absolute identification. The meaning will be, as Neill Q. Hamilton puts it, 'the Spirit so effectively performs His office of communicating to men the benefits of the risen Christ that for all intents and purposes of faith the Lord Himself is present bestowing grace on His own. The Spirit brings the ascended Lord to earth again'.[1] It must never be forgotten that the ministry of the Spirit is bound up inseparably with that of the Son. Under these circumstances the language of identification is understandable.

We see, then, that there is nothing in the objections that are usually raised to disturb our previous conclusions. The witness of the New Testament is clear enough. The Spirit is thought of consistently as a Person, and as a Person in some sense distinct from, though closely related to, the Father and the Son. The Spirit must not be thought of as a vague force or effluence. Nor is He another name for one aspect of the Father or the Son. He is a Person in His own right, with His own functions.

[1] *The Holy Spirit and Eschatology in Paul*, Edinburgh (London), 1957, p. 6. He cites Windisch and Buechsel as maintaining that the passage speaks of a 'dynamic identification' which he explains as one 'which occurs in redemptive action'. It is an identity of action, not of being.

CHAPTER IV

THE SPIRIT OF GOD

FEW people, I imagine, would think of the Spirit as a Person and deny that He is God. Historically, those who followed the heresy of Macedonius achieved this feat. But this seems to have been the result, not of an intelligently worked-out system of Christian doctrine, but of an unintelligent attempt at compromise following the overthrow of Arianism. Arius had denied the deity of the Son and of the Spirit. When his system was rejected by the Church, some of his followers said in effect, 'We would like to be reconciled to the Church. Why not meet us half way? We will accept the deity of the Son if you will deny that of the Spirit!' This may be good politics, but it is bad doctrine. Macedonianism was a danger for a time, but it did not really take long for it to be shown up as completely untenable. It has no real basis.

The real question in the doctrine of the Spirit is the question of personality. Once it is conceded that the Spirit is indeed a Person, and not an influence, a force, a stream, a thing, then it seems impossible to place Him on any level less than that of deity. A Personality such as this must necessarily be divine. However, for the sake of completeness we shall notice briefly the scriptural evidence for the deity of the Spirit, and then reflect on the considerable importance of this fact.

ASSOCIATION WITH THE FATHER AND THE SON

We have already noticed that there are several passages in the New Testament where the Spirit is mentioned in the closest of connections with the Father and the Son. Nothing is said in these passages about the relationship between the Three. Yet much is implied, as we will see if we examine them.

Let us take, for example, the baptismal saying: 'Go ye therefore, and make disciples of all the nations, baptizing them into the name of the Father and of the Son and of the Holy Ghost' (Mt. xxviii. 19). No affirmation is made about the essential nature of each of these. There is no definition of Godhead or the like. Yet that Godhead is implied we may see in a moment if we try the experiment of substituting the name of any created being in place of that of the Spirit. The archangel Michael, for all his dignity, sounds incongruous in such a place. As soon as we try to put anyone else there, we see the impossibility of such a procedure. The Three who are named are clearly commensurate with each other. No other could possibly be mentioned with Them.

Nor should we overlook the fact that the 'name' is singular. We might have expected 'names'. The singular further emphasizes the unity of the three Persons. While in some sense distinct, They are also in some sense one. Which is only another way of saying that the Spirit, as well as the Father and the Son, partakes in the nature of Deity.

The same procedure may be applied to all of the other sayings which connect the three Persons. All imply that the Spirit is a Being such as the others. And some of them add to this general inference. For example, when we read that the Spirit descended upon Jesus at His baptism (Mk. i. 10f.), we see that the Spirit is involved in the inauguration of the ministry of Jesus. It gives Him a special place in the working out of the incarnation (cf. also the references to Mary as being 'with child of the Holy Ghost', Mt. i. 18, 20; Lk. i. 35). Similarly a number of the passages in John picture the Spirit as pointing men to the Son, as witnessing to Him, as continuing His work (Jn. xiv. 26, xv. 26, xvi. 13–15). The close connection between the Spirit and the Son which we investigated at the beginning of the last chapter shows that the Spirit is more than a created being.

Paul has a somewhat similar thought in Romans xv. 16. He is talking about his preaching of the gospel and speaks of the Gentiles as 'being sanctified by the Holy Ghost'. The gospel of what Christ has done for men includes a place for the work of the Spirit. If anything, it is even more important that Paul speaks of the work of the Father in quickening men as done 'through his Spirit that dwelleth in you' (Rom. viii. 11).

We will not labour the point. The regular association of the Spirit with the Father and the Son clearly points to His being regarded as commensurate with Them. And the nature of His activities in conjunction with Them emphasizes His divine stature.

GOD WITHIN US

The thought that God is not some lofty and remote Being, but that in His love and His mercy He comes and dwells with man, is found throughout Holy Scripture. 'For thus saith the high and lofty One that inhabiteth eternity, whose name is Holy: I dwell in the high and holy place, with him also that is of a contrite and humble spirit' (Is. lvii. 15). This is one of the very precious truths to the saints of God.

Now sometimes it is made clear that it is as the Spirit that God dwells with and in men. Thus Paul can write to the Corinthians: 'Know ye not that ye are a temple of God, and that the Spirit of God dwelleth in you? . . . the temple of God is holy, which temple ye are' (1 Cor. iii. 16f.). The characteristic of a temple, of course, is that it is in a particular sense set apart for God. It is the place where men seek God's presence. It is the place where God dwells. And in this verse, immediately after saying that believers are 'a temple of God', Paul goes on to affirm that it is 'the Spirit of God' who dwells within. The inference is inescapable. The Spirit is God, God as He dwells in men. Paul returns to the same idea a few chapters later, when he asks, 'know ye not that your body is a temple of the Holy Ghost which is in you?' (1 Cor. vi.19). The difference is that in the earlier passage he has thought of the Spirit as dwelling within the Church, whereas here his thought is that the Spirit dwells within the believer. But for our present purpose both passages say the same thing: the Spirit is the divine within us. The Spirit is God as He dwells within men.

John quotes from some words of Jesus that make it clear

that this is no temporary phenomenon. On the last night before the crucifixion Jesus said to His apostles, 'I will pray the Father, and he shall give you another Comforter, that he may be with you for ever, even the Spirit of truth' (Jn. xiv. 16f.). The manifestation of which we have just been thinking is not some fleeting and casual affair. The Spirit's presence within men is 'for ever'.

When we come to think of the work of the Spirit among men we will be thinking of some of the consequences of all this. Here it is sufficient to notice that that Spirit, who dwells within men as in a temple, and whose sanctifying presence will never be withdrawn, cannot be less than God.

THE DEEP THINGS OF GOD

There is a somewhat perplexing reference to the Spirit in a passage where Paul is concerned with revelation. The Spirit reveals to us certain things, he says, and then goes on, 'For who among men knoweth the things of a man, save the spirit of the man, which is in him? even so the things of God none knoweth, save the Spirit of God' (1 Cor. ii. 11). The analogy of man's nature is here the key to the understanding of certain truths concerning the Spirit. Only the man himself knows what goes on inside a man.

One of the beautiful things about a sermon or a lecture from the point of view of the hearer (and one of the tragic ones from that of the speaker) is that, if you find it uninteresting, you don't have to take it in. In thought you can be miles away in pleasanter regions by far, though outwardly it may seem that you are paying rapt attention. Other people, looking at you from the outside, can never really know what is going on inside you. They may guess, sometimes fairly accurately, but they cannot *know*. Only your spirit, which is inside you, knows. In like manner, reasons Paul, no man can know what goes on inside the divine nature. 'The deep things of God' belong to God alone, and man can enter into them only to the extent that God is pleased to disclose them. But the Spirit is not limited as man is. The Spirit knows God from within,

so to speak. He shares in the nature of Deity, and so the deep
things of God are plain and open to Him.

The same truth is expressed otherwise in other parts of the
New Testament. For example, prophecy is explained this
way: 'men spake from God, being moved by the Holy
Ghost' (2 Pet. i. 21). The prophets were men who declared
the authentic word of God. They did this, not because they
were especially shrewd fellows, nor because they had outstanding wisdom or spirituality or insight. They did it because
the Holy Spirit 'moved' them (perhaps better, 'carried them
along'). The Holy Spirit, in other words, knowing the inner
secrets of God, inspired the prophets. What no created
being could ever find out for himself the Spirit imparted to
them.

BLASPHEMY AGAINST THE HOLY SPIRIT

There is a saying of Jesus, reported in all three Synoptic
Gospels, in which blasphemy against the Spirit is regarded
as the most heinous of all sins (Mt. xii. 31f.; Mk. iii. 28f.;
Lk. xii. 10). All three agree that this is the most serious of all
sins, and Matthew and Luke specifically say that it is worse
than blasphemy against the Son of man.

This saying has caused a great deal of difficulty to very
many, so that it may be as well to say a little about it. The sin
is not closely defined, but it is plain that Jesus does not refer
to the uttering of a few idle or slanderous words only.
Blasphemy may be in act, as well as in word. Jesus is referring
to a whole attitude of life. Matthew and Mark tell us that the
occasion of the saying was an accusation by the opponents of
Jesus that He cast out devils by the prince of the devils. In
other words, they deliberately ascribed His deeds of mercy,
deeds done in the power of the Holy Spirit, to an evil agency.
They chose to call good, evil. To take up this position was to
reject all that Jesus stood for. Moreover, as the Spirit is
especially characteristic of the new life Christ came to bring,
to sin against the Spirit in this way means to reject that new

life.[1] Bavinck speaks of this sin as 'a sin against the Gospel in its clearest revelation', a sin which consists 'not in doubting or simply denying the truth, but in a denial which goes against the conviction of the intellect, against the enlightenment of conscience, against the dictates of the heart; in a conscious, wilful and intentional imputation to the influence and working of Satan of that which is clearly recognized as God's work, i.e. in a definite blasphemy of the Holy Ghost, in a wilful declaration that the Holy Ghost is the Spirit from the abyss, that truth is a lie, and that Christ is Satan himself'.[2] It is important to be clear on this. There is an attitude of life that rebels against what the Spirit reveals, that calls good evil, that turns its back on the highest and best. It is a persistent rejection of the Spirit of God. It is a solemn and searching thought that if this is a man's attitude, there is no forgiveness for him.

For our present purpose the emphasis must be on the place that the saying gives to the Spirit. If to blaspheme Him is to commit the unforgivable sin, if to blaspheme Him is worse than to blaspheme the Son of man (whom Christians hold to be certainly divine), then clearly the Spirit is God. Nothing less will meet the situation.

A confirmation of the high place that this gives the Spirit is to be seen in other sayings which concern the Spirit and the Son. Thus early in Jesus' ministry we are told that 'the Spirit driveth him forth into the wilderness' (Mk. i. 12), which on any showing does not make the Spirit less than the Son.

---

[1] This is important. Sometimes one meets troubled souls who feel that some word or words they have spoken, or some particular action they have done, constitutes the unforgivable sin. But it is a whole attitude that is in question, nothing less. Alan Richardson reminds us that 'to reject the inbreaking Aeon (the Kingdom of God) and to dismiss the signs of its arrival—such as the exorcisms which demonstrate the overthrow of Satan's counter-kingdom—as the work of Beelzebub, is to reject the salvation which God is bringing and is in fact to be guilty of unforgivable sin against the New Age' (*An Introduction to the Theology of the New Testament*, London, 1958, p. 108). This, and not some smaller thing, is the blasphemy of which Jesus speaks.

[2] Cited by N. Geldenhuys, *Commentary on the Gospel of Luke*, London, 1952, p. 352. Geldenhuys goes on to say, 'Using Platonic terminology, we may call it "the lie in the soul" '.

Similarly the descent of the Spirit upon Jesus at the beginning of His ministry, and His quotation from Isaiah in the synagogue at Nazareth ('The Spirit of the Lord is upon me, because he anointed me to preach good tidings to the poor', Lk. iv. 18), combine to emphasize that the earthly ministry was in the power of and under the guidance of the Spirit. If we think of Jesus as divine, then the conclusion is inescapable: we must think of the Spirit also as divine.

DIVINE ATTRIBUTES

Throughout the New Testament divine attributes are freely ascribed to the Spirit. Thus just as God is thought of as omnipresent, so is it with the Spirit. 'For in one Spirit were we all baptized into one body, whether Jews or Greeks, whether bond or free; and were all made to drink of one Spirit' (1 Cor. xii. 13). The Spirit must be in every place in order to discharge such functions. Similarly we see that omniscience belongs to the Spirit from the passage on 'the deep things of God' that we were discussing in an earlier section (1 Cor. ii. 10ff.). Nothing, not even those things that belong to the innermost nature of God, is hid from Him. It may be that omnipotence is being ascribed to Him in such passages as Romans xv. 19, 'in the power of signs and wonders, in the power of the Holy Ghost', or in 1 Corinthians xii. 11 which speaks of the Spirit giving His gifts 'to each one severally even as he will'. At the very least no-one and nothing is thought of as being able to hinder Him in doing such things. The ability to save, which is everywhere ascribed to Him (e.g. Rom. viii. 2, 11; Tit. iii. 5), may also be thought of in the same way. In the Old Testament it is the prerogative of God to bring salvation to His people.

With this we should place those passages wherein the Spirit is said to be the Author of holy Scripture, such as Acts i. 16: 'it was needful that the scripture should be fulfilled, which the Holy Ghost spake before by the mouth of David . . .' Especially important is such a passage as Hebrews x. 15, 'And the Holy Ghost also beareth witness . . .' For when we look up the passage quoted (Je. xxxi. 33) we find that the words there are the words of the Lord. Similarly, 'wherewith your fathers tempted me' in Hebrews iii. 9 is introduced by 'even as the Holy Ghost saith' (verse 7). But in Exodus xvii. 7 (which refers to the kind of incident in mind) 'they tempted the Lord' refers to God. Clearly the Spirit is thought of as God in the fullest sense. Indeed, this conclusion springs out of the fact that the Spirit is said to be the Author of Scripture. Nowadays there are many who think of the Bible as basically the product of men, albeit Spirit-inspired men. Others think of a mixture, great divine truths being expressed in imperfect human words, thus allowing for human errors. But these are modern ideas. In the first century those who used the Old Testament were quite sure that it was the utterance of God. To say that the Holy Ghost originated it was thus the same thing as to say that He was God.

The process comes to its logical conclusion when the Spirit is explicitly said to be God. Peter, speaking to Ananias, says, 'why hath Satan filled thy heart to lie to the Holy Ghost . . ? thou hast not lied unto men, but unto God' (Acts v. 3–5).

There is thus an abundance of evidence that the Spirit is thought of as divine. Yet even so we must not think that the conclusion depends only on the passages cited. They are, I imagine, sufficient; but we must bear in mind, as Swete says, that 'the divinity of the Spirit does not rest on isolated sayings; it is involved in the view which is given of the Spirit's work considered as a whole'.[1]

And this is of tremendous importance. When we know that the power that comes into our hearts and lives as we become Christians is not the power of any creature, but that of none less than God Himself, then that makes all the difference. To be closely allied to an angelic being is one thing. To have first-hand experience of a cosmic force might be little more. But to know the power and the continuing presence of God Himself is another and a very different matter indeed.

[1] *The Holy Spirit in the New Testament*, London, 1910, p. 289.

CHAPTER V

THE SPIRIT IN THE CHURCH

I T is somewhat arbitrary to distinguish between what the Spirit does in the Church, and what He does in the believer, for neither exists without the other. The believer is necessarily a church member. As 'a serious man' said to John Wesley, 'Remember you cannot serve Him alone; you must, therefore, find companions, or make them; the Bible knows nothing of solitary religion.'[1] And the Church is obviously composed of believers. There is no Church apart from men of faith. Nevertheless it is convenient in a study such as ours to treat separately those activities of the Spirit which primarily concern the Church and those which are more immediately relevant to the individual believer. First then let us look at the Spirit in the corporate life of the Church.

THE DAY OF PENTECOST

In the second chapter of Acts we read of a series of extraordinary happenings. The disciples 'were all together in one place' (verse 1) on the day of Pentecost, when suddenly they heard a sound, which they likened to that of a mighty wind. It seemed to fill the whole house in which they were. They also saw something unusual. It was like fiery tongues parting asunder and coming to rest on the members of the little band.

These physical phenomena were not all nor even the most important of the things that happened that day. The disciples felt themselves to be new men. The very Spirit of God was within them, and that to an unusual degree. They were 'filled

[1] J. Telford, *The Life of John Wesley*, London, 1910, p. 147. Cf. also W. H. Griffith Thomas, 'It must be constantly borne in mind that the true, full, vigorous, mature Christian life is impossible to any Christian who tries to live a solitary life' (*The Holy Spirit of God*, London, 1913, p. 176).

with the Holy Spirit' (verse 4). In an earlier chapter we noticed that when the Spirit came upon men in the Old Testament there were sometimes unusual accompaniments, and that was so here also. The disciples 'began to speak with other tongues' (verse 4), the meaning of which appears to be that no matter where people came from they were able to understand what was said (verses 7–11). It is noteworthy also that the disciples, who appear to have been hiding away from their enemies in the spirit of John xx. 19, immediately became different people. They unlocked their door, and went down to the most public place they could find and there preached Jesus boldly. This change from cringing cowards to fearless preachers was permanent. We read of Christians making all sorts of mistakes afterwards, and they are far from being perfect. But we do not again read of them hiding away for fear of men. The Spirit altered all that. From now on they became fearless vehicles of the Spirit in proclaiming to men the message of the gospel.

L. S. Thornton brings out the significance of Pentecost in this way. 'When the Spirit was given then their (i.e. the disciples') minds were illuminated with the full truth of God's love in Christ. Pentecost presupposed Calvary and could have had no distinctive meaning without Calvary. Yet the meaning of Calvary became accessible only through the outpouring of the Spirit at Pentecost.

'Pentecost brought' an illumination of the mind which transformed their outlook. Everything looked different, as everything looks different when a drought is followed by a shower of rain. The very rays of the sun seem different in such circumstances! The rays which were scorching are now pleasantly warming. All the details of nature are the same; yet all have been transformed. So it was after Pentecost. The souls of the disciples were like watered gardens. With the descending streams of the Spirit came the revelation of God's love. The truth for which their souls thirsted now refreshed them.'[1]

On that day of Pentecost Peter was the chief speaker. A

[1] *The Common Life in the Body of Christ*, London, 1944, p. 104.

report of his sermon is given in Acts ii. As H. B. Swete reminds us, his words show 'a blending of courage, wisdom, and skill which we do not associate with him as he appears in the Gospels, and an insight into the work of the Messiah and the nature of His Kingdom such as even to the last day of the Lord's stay upon earth was certainly beyond his reach'.[1] Moreover this was not confined to Peter. 'From that day forward a new strength, which was not their own, marked all the sayings and deeds of the Apostolic Church.'[2]

At the end of Peter's sermon many of his hearers were convicted of their sinfulness and of their need. They asked direction of the speaker, who told them to repent and be baptized, when they, too, would receive the gift of the Holy Spirit. The result was that three thousand souls were added to the Church of God (verse 41). This meant more than standing up and being counted, as the close of the narrative plainly shows. The new converts remained in the fellowship. They studied the teaching (or doctrine) of the apostles. They joined in 'the breaking of bread' (which is almost certainly the service of Holy Communion), and in 'the prayers' (about which it is not easy to be specific, though the general idea is plain enough).

Some refer to these happenings as 'the birthday of the Church'. Here everything depends on what you mean by 'the birthday'. In one sense the Church may be said to have begun way back in the days of the Old Testament, when God first brought His people into covenant with Himself. In another sense it began when the first disciples heard Jesus say 'Follow me', and they left all and followed Him. In another sense it began when Peter made his great confession of faith and heard Jesus say, 'upon this rock I will build my church' (Mt. xvi. 18). In yet another sense it began on Calvary when that atonement was wrought that would do away with men's sins and make them the children of God.

But in the full sense of the Church in vigorous life, redeemed by the cross of Christ, invigorated by the divine

[1] *The Holy Spirit in the New Testament*, London, 1910, p. 76.
[2] *Ibid.*, pp. 76f.

power, set forth on the path of work and worship, the Church certainly did not come into existence until that day of Pentecost. The coming of the Spirit upon the little band of disciples galvanized them into action. It constituted them as the Church. And the Church is never really the Church when it is out of communion with what happened at Pentecost. It is only as it is filled with the Holy Spirit of God that the Church can be said to be the Church in any meaningful sense.

Pentecost represents God's decisive gift. Sometimes people sigh for, or pray for 'another Pentecost'. They might as well pray for 'another crucifixion'. Each represents a divine action which brooks no repetition. At Pentecost God gave the Spirit to the Church in full measure. The gift has never been withdrawn.

THE 'VICAR' OF CHRIST

In an arresting phrase the early Christian writer Tertullian speaks of Christ as sending the Holy Spirit to be His 'Vicar'.[1] To get the force of this we must bear in mind that with us the words 'Vicar' and 'Curate' have exchanged their meanings. Properly speaking, the 'Curate' is the man who is charged with the 'cure' or care of souls. His 'Vicar' is his deputy who takes his place when he cannot be there. In accordance with the original and proper meaning of the term, then, Tertullian thinks of the Spirit as Christ's 'Vicar', as the One who takes the place of Christ now that the period of His ministry among men is over.

During the days of His flesh the visible presence of the Master heartened and inspired His followers. But at the end He told them plainly, 'It is expedient for you that I go away' (Jn. xvi. 7). He added that if He did not go away, the Spirit would not come. Why this should be we do not know. We may hazard the conjecture that the inner presence of the Spirit within men is not compatible with an external presence of the incarnate Son. But, whether we are right or wrong, what the Lord was making clear is that the Spirit's presence

[1] *De praescr.* 13.

is something supremely to be desired. Probably most
Christians at one time or another have thought: 'Would it
not be wonderful to have been in Palestine during the time
of our Lord! To have seen Him as He went about doing good.
To have heard Him as He uttered His matchless parables. To
have had close and immediate contact with the Lord Himself.'
But Jesus tells us that we have in point of fact something that
is better even than that. We have the presence of God the
Holy Spirit within our hearts.

The Church, then, in the post-incarnation period is not
bereft of the divine presence. Though her Master ascended
into heaven where He was before, He did not leave her
comfortless or defenceless. The living presence of the Spirit
is the assurance that He still supplies her every need.

And it is a living presence. The divine Spirit is active and
sovereign in the Church. This is obscured in the way some
'catholics' understand the situation. They put all the stress on
the Church as the dispenser of the sacraments, and thus more
or less put her in charge of the gifts of the Spirit. Bishop Gore
speaks of 'the "tying" of grace to sacraments in the Church'.[1]
In summing up the argument of his book he refers to 'the
one visible society as the only covenanted sphere of Christ's
redemption. . . . The principle of the sacraments we saw to be
that they are social ceremonies, in which the grace of the
Spirit is attached at point after point to the community life'.[2]
Despite the title of his book, there are large stretches with no
mention of the Spirit at all. The Church is clearly primary.
George S. Hendry similarly complains that in the Roman
Church 'the power and authority, which derive from the
Holy Spirit, are held to be given to the Church itself to
exercise'.[3]

[1] *The Holy Spirit and the Church*, London, 1924, p. 27.
[2] *Op. cit.*, p. 342. Cf. 'the religion of the Spirit was membership in a
society which had authoritative rulers' (*op. cit.*, p. 167).
[3] *The Holy Spirit in Christian Theology*, London, 1957, p. 56. Cf. also
J. E. Fison, the 'catholic' view of church and sacrament 'renders
inevitable the most searching examination as to whether in reality any
room is left for an adequate recognition of the Third Person of the
Trinity' (*The Blessing of the Holy Spirit*, London, 1950, p. 12).

But in the New Testament the Church is not the important thing, directing and channelling the gifts of the Spirit where it wills. It is impossible to think of any man or any group of men, even the Church, as being put in charge of the Spirit. Geddes MacGregor pertinently asks, 'Can there be a custodianship of the Spirit?'[1] The answer to the question cannot be in doubt. The Church is subject to the Spirit. The Protestant position is truer to the New Testament when it affirms that the Spirit 'makes his indwelling presence known, not by inflating the Church with a sense of its own privilege and power, but by directing its attention to its living and exalted Lord and by exposing it to his grace'.[2] The Spirit, not the Church, is supreme. 'He that hath an ear, let him hear what the Spirit saith to the churches' runs like a refrain through the second and third chapters of Revelation. And it reminds us of the dynamic presence of the living Spirit of God in the true Church.

THE FELLOWSHIP OF THE SPIRIT

In two places in the New Testament we read of the 'fellowship of the Spirit' (2 Cor. xiii. 14, where the word translated 'communion' means 'fellowship', and Phil. ii. 1). It is possible to engage in some delightfully abstract disputes about the finer points of Greek grammar (muttering learnedly about 'subjective' and 'objective' genitives), and to discuss whether the primary meaning here is 'participation in the Spirit' or 'fellowship created by the Spirit'. But we eschew such delights, merely stopping to point out that both ideas are true, and that in all probability the latter is the one that is meant. Thus R. V. G. Tasker explains the expression as pointing to 'that fellowship which the Holy Spirit creates

---

[1] *Corpus Christi*, London, 1959, p. 213. He also points out that 'The doctrine of the Reformed tradition implies a protest against the notion that the Spirit might ever be "conserved" in an "organ" within the Body, and against the view that it can be given to any man, or even to the ministry as a whole, to be the curator of the Spirit' (*op. cit.*, p. 212).

[2] G. S. Hendry, *op. cit.*, p. 66.

among all who have stood beneath the cross and accepted
Christ as their personal Saviour'.[1] If, with L. S. Thornton, we
adopt the former as the meaning, then as that writer says, 'it
must not be understood in a sense which excludes the other
alternative. The two interpretations emphasize two aspects of
a complex whole which includes them both'.[2]

Whatever be the verdict on the disputed point it is beyond
doubt that the New Testament views the Christian Church
as a fellowship of the redeemed, and a fellowship created by
the Holy Spirit. It is not simply the result of the coming
together of like-minded people, drawn together by a common interest. It is the result of the action of the Spirit Himself.
Throughout the New Testament the Church appears as a
Spirit-filled and Spirit-indwelt body. No amount of the
energy of the flesh can produce the Church of God. Only the
divine within can do that. And wherever there is a Church,
the true Church, there there will always be the activity of the
very Spirit of God Himself. The Church does not go its own
sweet way. It is created by the Spirit. It is indwelt by the
Spirit. It is the fellowship of the Spirit. It goes where the
Spirit leads. The Christian life is characterized by a peculiar
quality, the indwelling of God. It derives its life unceasingly
from Him, and where this has ceased to be the truth, there the
Church exists no longer.

This marks an advance on the teaching of the Old Testament. There the Spirit came upon selected individuals equip-
ping them for specific tasks. Here the Spirit comes upon the
Church as such. The Church is the community of the Spirit.
'The Pauline understanding of the Spirit makes Him the key
to the understanding both of the gospel and of the Church.
For the realization of the Spirit is pre-eminently, as Pentecost
demonstrates, not in man as an individual, but between man
and man in the distinctive "fellowship" that He creates and
sustains.'[3] While the Spirit of the Lord was active in ancient

[1] *Tyndale Commentary* on 2 Cor. xiii. 14.
[2] *The Common Life in the Body of Christ*, London, 1944, p. 74.
[3] J. E. Fison, *op. cit.*, p. 130.

Israel, one would not spontaneously refer to that community as 'the community of the Spirit'. But this is a very apt description of the Church of the New Testament.

In line with this the unity that binds believers together is sometimes expressed in terms of the Spirit. For example, we are exhorted to 'keep the unity of the Spirit in the bond of peace' (Eph. iv. 3), and we are reminded that 'there is one body and one Spirit' (Eph. iv. 4). The unity that unites Christians is not man-made (though it may be man-destroyed). It depends on supernatural activity of the Spirit.

WORSHIP

We are accustomed to thinking of worship as an activity of the spirit of man. And so it is. But it is an exciting thought that it is also an activity of the Spirit of God. 'We are the circumcision (i.e. the true people of God),' says Paul, 'who worship by the Spirit of God' (Phil. iii. 3). That is to say, the distinguishing mark of God's people is the particular way in which they worship, namely 'by the Spirit'. When Christians worship, the Spirit of God permeates the whole, guiding and directing His people. Since God is spirit, 'they that worship him must worship in spirit and truth' (Jn. iv. 24). This means primarily that true worship is spiritual. But it opens the way to the thought which we have seen is explicit in Paul, that it is only as the very Spirit of God is in our worship that we may worship acceptably. In the words of H. B. Swete: 'the spiritual worship which is claimed demands a spiritual force which is not innate in man; to worship in spirit and truth is possible only through the Spirit of God'.[1]

The Spirit's activity is explicitly connected with prayer in Ephesians vi. 18: 'with all prayer and supplication praying at all seasons in the Spirit'. Prayer in the strength of man is an intermittent affair at best. But 'in the Spirit' it will continue 'at all seasons'. Prayer carried out as a human activity is a barren and lifeless affair. But when the Spirit of God is at

---

[1] *The Holy Spirit in the New Testament*, London, 1910, p. 139.

work in the prayer, the situation is transformed. Prayer then becomes a mighty force, breaking down strongholds.

Prayer all too often is half-hearted. But Paul beseeches the Romans 'by the love of the Spirit, that ye strive together with me in your prayers to God for me' (Rom. xv. 30). His verb is *sunagōnizomai* which conveys the idea of strenuous effort, even of wrestling in prayer (the uncompounded verb *agōnizomai* is the usual verb for competing in a contest at the Olympic Games). The love of the Spirit fills our prayers with life and warmth. They become real spiritual exercises.

We get further light on this in the passage in Romans where Paul is dwelling on human limitations in prayer. 'The Spirit', he says, 'also helpeth our infirmity: for we know not how to pray as we ought; but the Spirit himself maketh intercession for us with groanings which cannot be uttered' (Rom. viii. 26). AV reads 'we know not what we should pray for', but this is not the thought. It is the manner, not the matter of our prayer that is meant. (It is true that we do not know our basic needs, and therefore need guidance as to what to pray for, but that is not being dealt with here.) There are times when we would pray, but the words will not come. We feel deeply the need of prayer, but the best we can produce is 'groanings'. Even at such times we need not despair. The Spirit uses those very inarticulate cries. He is in them, and makes intercession for us. He conveys to the Father the meaning we cannot.

Another illuminating passage is the opening chapter of Revelation. Here John introduces his book and he tells us that the vision of God came to him as he was 'in the Spirit on the Lord's day' (verse 10). He makes it clear that he was a 'partaker . . . in the tribulation' and that he was in exile on Patmos (verse 9). But even there the servant of God at worship can rise above his circumstances and see visions of God. The same experience is used of John's seeing the very throne of God and Him that sat on it (Rev. iv. 2, cf. xvii. 3, xxi. 10). It is very instructive as to the method and results of true worship.

Scripture thus has a good deal to say about prayer *in* the

Spirit. Before we leave the subject it may be as well to add a note on prayer *to* the Spirit. This must be regarded as legitimate. If we accept the deity of the Spirit, then we cannot forbid prayer to Him. And in point of fact the Christian Church has always engaged in such prayer to some extent. We still do it in some of our hymns (e.g. 'Spirit Divine, attend our prayers'). We find it in the petition in the Prayer Book Litany which reads, 'O God the Holy Ghost, proceeding from the Father and the Son: have mercy upon us. . . .' The Nicene Creed gives the justification for all this when it speaks of the Spirit as 'the Lord and giver of life, . . . who with the Father and the Son together is worshipped . . .'

Yet the practice has never become the Church's rule. Always prayers to the Spirit have been exceptional. It is the Christian custom to address prayer to the Father. This is the scriptural habit. There is no example in the Bible of prayer addressed to the Spirit.[1] There no-one speaks to Him. There His function is not to act as the Receiver of prayer, but rather to bear witness to Christ. As J. B. Green puts it, this 'is in beautiful harmony with what Christ in His farewell discourse said about the mission of the Spirit. His mission is to point to another'.[2] The New Testament is a Christocentric book. Our prayers should be based on that fact.

THE SPIRITUAL GIFTS

It is a moot point whether we should treat certain gifts of the Spirit bestowed upon individuals under the heading of 'The Work of the Spirit in the Believer' or under our present heading. I choose to deal with the subject here, because, although the gifts are certainly individual, the New Testament stresses that they are given within the Church, and with a view to building up the Church.

---

[1] J. Elder Cumming thinks that 'The threefold Benediction partakes of the nature of prayer, and may be said to be offered to each of the Three Persons' (*Through the Eternal Spirit*, London, n.d., p. 87). But this is very indirect, and Cumming admits the 'absence in the New Testament of *direct prayer* to Him' (*loc. cit.*; Cumming's italics).

[2] *Studies in the Holy Spirit*, Weaverville, N.C., 1957, p. 73.

The word Paul uses for the 'gifts' is *charisma* (plural *charismata*). This word is connected with *charis*, 'grace', and stresses that the 'gifts' come of the Spirit's free bounty. They are not bestowed as a result of human merit or human seeking. No man, for example, decides that he will be a prophet. Either God gives him the gift of prophecy or He does not. And so with other gifts.

There are four principal passages which deal with the 'gifts': Romans xii. 6–8; I Corinthians xii. 4–11, 28–31; I Corinthians xiv. 1ff.; Ephesians iv. 7–12. In each case the thought of gift is prominent, and in each case the gift is exercised in community. From the Romans passage we find that all Christians have gifts, different gifts. Each should exercise the gift that God has given him. The same thought recurs in I Corinthians xii, where the illustration is used of the differing functions of the various parts of the body. In this chapter the important principle is laid down that the test of any who claims to have the Spirit is his attitude to Christ. If he gives due place to the lordship of Christ the Holy Spirit is inspiring him. If he does not, then he has not the Spirit (verse 3).

Later in the chapter several 'gifts' are mentioned, as 'the word of wisdom', 'the word of knowledge', 'faith', 'gifts of healings', 'workings of miracles', 'prophecy', 'discernings of spirits', 'divers kinds of tongues', and 'the interpretation of tongues' (verses 8–10). Towards the end of the chapter we have a list of those whom God has 'set . . . in the church'. The order is apostles, prophets, teachers, miracles, gifts of healings, helps, governments, divers kinds of tongues (verse 28). In a series of questions which follows Paul adds another gift, the interpretation of tongues.

The gift of tongues is treated at greater length in chapter xiv. In Ephesians, five gifts only are mentioned: apostles, prophets, evangelists, pastors and teachers (Eph. iv. 11; the last two may perhaps be a unity).

The reason for these gifts of the Spirit is made clear in Ephesians. There we read that God gave them 'for the perfecting of the saints, unto the work of ministering, unto the building up of the body of Christ' (Eph. iv. 12). In other words, God, who has called the Church into being, has equipped various members of it with the gifts needed to build it up into that maturity that He purposes for it. The gifts are not given purely for the personal enjoyment of their possessors. They are meant to be used in the service of the Church, the beloved community.

Concerning some of the gifts there is not much dispute. We know so much about apostles from the New Testament generally that we need not feel that their main functions are hid from us. So with the prophets. But it is not so with all the gifts. Take, for example, the 'helps' and 'governments' of I Corinthians xii. 28. We may make more or less learned conjectures based on the etymology of the words, on their usage in Greek generally, on our knowledge of the early Church, or on our own personal idiosyncrasies. But when we boil it all down, we *know* nothing about these gifts or their possessors. They have vanished without leaving visible trace. Concerning others we must adopt an intermediate position. Thus we know pretty well what the meaning of 'teachers' is, in our sense of the term, and it may be that this corresponds fairly closely to the 'teachers' under discussion. Though, if so, it is difficult to see why a special 'gift' of the Spirit was needed, and we are left with the uncomfortable feeling that maybe there is more in this than meets the eye. So with 'faith' (I Cor. xii. 9). We all know what faith means. But does 'faith' in this context mean the usual kind of faith? If so, why is it regarded as a special gift given to some people and not to others? The faith we know of is the *sine qua non* for being a Christian.

It is important that we should realize that these doubts and obscurities exist. The early Church knew quite well what all these gifts were. They exulted in the exercise of them. But, in view of the fact that they disappeared so speedily and so completely that we do not even know for certain exactly what they were, we must regard them as the gift of God for the time of the Church's infancy. They did not last for very long, and in the providence of God evidently they were not expected to last for very long.[1] In those early days there was the outpouring of the Spirit of God to supply every need of the infant community. And some of those needs were not our needs. It is to this, I think, that we must ascribe the fact that some if not all of the *charismata* vanished with the early Church. God still supplies all the needs of His people, but those needs do not necessarily require the *charismata* of New Testament days.

This must be said, because there are people today who hold that some of the *charismata* are a necessity for Christians who are loyal to the New Testament. Particularly is this so with the gift of 'tongues'. We are somewhat in the dark about this gift, but it appears to have been the gift of speech in a rather ecstatic fashion such that the speaker did not understand what he was saying (unless he had that other gift of interpretation).[2] Some Christians claim that this gift has never been withdrawn from the Church, and that it still may and should be exercised. There is something of a tendency to look down on those who have not received this gift, or at least to regard their experience of the Holy Spirit as deficient.[3] 'Tongues' are thought to be evidence of the 'baptism of the Spirit'. The position is supported by drawing attention to three passages wherein the gift of the Spirit was accompanied by 'tongues' (Acts ii. 1–4, x. 44–46, xix. 1–6; it should not be overlooked,

---

[1] Dr. Graham Scroggie says 'the extraordinary manifestations of the Spirit during the Apostolic age, manifestations which were clearly evidential, served the purpose of inaugurating the Christian dispensation and were then withdrawn' (*The Baptism of the Spirit and Speaking with Tongues*, London, n.d., p. 22). Cf. also W. G. Young, 'The early church did not have the New Testament; it did not have centuries of Christian experience: it was new. It needed certain gifts which we do not now need in the same way' (*The Life of Faith*, June 5, 1958, p. 381).

[2] See further, *Tyndale Commentary* on 1 Cor. xii. 10.

[3] Cyril H. Maskrey, formerly an Apostolic Pastor and 'Apostle', says that 'the dogmatic denominational presentation of Pentecostalism' officially says 'Speaking in tongues is a pivotal doctrine in the Holy Ghost Movement . . . is not only AN evidence but is THE Bible evidence of the baptism of the Holy Spirit'. He adds 'It is further stated that one who has not spoken in tongues does not have the same power for service as one who has' (*The Pentecostal Error*, Adelaide, 1953, p. 1).

however, that on other occasions no such manifestation is mentioned, Acts viii. 17, ix. 17–19).

In the face of this attitude it must be insisted upon, in the first place, that the New Testament does not regard it as a gift given indiscriminately to all believers who seek it. Indeed, the 'to another' of 1 Corinthians xii. 10 seems to imply that there were some to whom the gift was not given. This is the natural way also of understanding 1 Corinthians xiv. And 'No' is the only possible answer to the question 'do all speak with tongues?' in 1 Corinthians xii. 30. Acts x. 44–46, xix. 1–6 point to a speaking with tongues that was not a permanent gift, but a phenomenon on the occasion of the reception of the Holy Spirit. But there is no indication that the same experience is expected to take place in the case of all others. We might just as much insist from Acts viii. 14–17 that a necessity for the reception of the Spirit is the laying on of hands of an apostle. It must not be overlooked that we have mention of speaking with 'tongues' at the reception of the Spirit on only three occasions, and each of these may fairly be regarded as exceptional. One of them was on the day of Pentecost (when the 'tongues' may have been different from those in the other examples; they appear to have been intelligible, whereas in the other cases they apparently were not), one was on the occasion of the admission of Gentiles to the Church, and the third took place in a group outside Palestine who had had moreover a defective understanding of Christianity. There is a discussion of 'tongues' in 1 Corinthians xiv, but outside the three passages mentioned no-one in the New Testament is actually said to have exercised the gift. This in itself should show that this gift was not the normal prerogative of all Christian people.

In the second place, historically all the gifts disappeared quite early in the history of the Church. It was not long before there were no apostles, prophets, and the rest. And, as we have pointed out already, some of the gifts disappeared so completely that to this day we do not know what they were. Even the gift of 'tongues' comes under this heading. Despite the confident claims of some, we cannot be certain of exactly what from the gift took in New Testament days. We cannot feel that the

Spirit of God would have allowed this state of affairs to develop and to continue if the gift were so important.

In the third place, the gift seems always to be associated with spiritual immaturity, not with spiritual maturity and stability. Paul could thank God that he possessed the gift in greater measure than others (1 Cor. xiv. 18). But there is no record of his ever exercising the gift, and he expressly tells us that he would sooner speak five intelligible words in church than ten thousand words in a 'tongue' (1 Cor. xiv. 19). Those of whom we read who spoke in 'tongues' were all recent converts. We need not doubt that the gift was a real gift from God. But it was a gift for the immature rather than the profound.

And in the fourth place, the test of the Spirit's presence in the New Testament is the glorification of Christ. It is only 'in the Holy Spirit' that the lordship of Christ can be confessed (1 Cor. xii. 3). W. H. Griffith Thomas once received a letter from a woman, saying: 'I have prayed, I have read the Bible, I have striven. I have done all that I can and I still am not sure whether I have the fullness of the Spirit.' 'Turn your thoughts out, not in,' replied the great theologian. 'What is Christ to you? If He is little you have not the fullness of the Spirit. If He is Chief among ten thousand and Altogether Lovely, you have the fullness of the Spirit.'

Along the same lines it is clear that the New Testament places ethical changes as the supreme evidence of the presence of the Spirit. Paul introduces his matchless discussion of love in 1 Corinthians xiii with 'and a still more excellent way shew I unto you' (1 Cor. xii. 31), 'more excellent', that is, than the way of 'tongues' and the like which have been mentioned in the previous verse. 'But the end of the charge is love out of a pure heart and a good conscience and faith unfeigned' (1 Tim. i. 5). As a modern poet puts it,

'Not where I breathe
But where I love, I live'.[1]

Love is the very central thing.

[1] Cited by F. W. Dillistone, *The Holy Spirit in the Life of Today*, London, 1946, p. 49. Dillistone adds, 'The Spirit manifests Himself first as life but finally as love'.

In all the excitement of dealing with the spectacular gifts we sometimes lose sight of the fact that the Spirit is at work in appointing the regular ministry of the Church. Paul spoke to the elders of Ephesus about 'the flock, in the which the Holy Ghost hath made you bishops' (Acts xx. 28). The reference to the 'gift' (*charisma*) that was given to Timothy 'by prophecy, with the laying on of the hands of the presbytery' (1 Tim. iv. 14) may point to the same thing. It is important to be clear that the power of ministry in a congregation is a gift of the Spirit of God.

THE EXTENSION OF THE CHURCH

The last command of our Saviour was that His followers should go into all the world and make disciples (Mt. xxviii. 19). This command He supplemented with the instruction that they were to wait in Jerusalem until they should receive 'the promise of the Father'. 'Ye shall be baptized with the Holy Ghost', He said (Acts i. 4f.). The point is made even more plain by His subsequent words, 'ye shall receive power, when the Holy Ghost is come upon you: and ye shall be my witnesses both in Jerusalem, and in all Judaea and Samaria, and unto the uttermost part of the earth' (Acts i. 8).

The position is plain. The disciples were commissioned to take the gospel throughout the whole wide world. They were to be the witnesses of their Master wherever they went. But the task was not one to be discharged in their own strength. To do it they would need the enduing of the Holy Spirit. So before they could go out they must wait for the promised gift of power. The gospel is not to be proclaimed other than under the direction of and in the strength of the Holy Spirit of God.

In the later parts of the Acts we see the working out of all this. The Holy Spirit galvanized the Church into activity, as is recorded in Acts ii. The Holy Spirit directed the 'prophets and teachers' at Antioch to separate Barnabas and Saul for the special work He had for them to do (Acts xiii. 1f.). These

two apostles accordingly can be said to have been 'sent forth
by the Holy Ghost' (Acts xiii. 4). Paul's first miracle of
judgment took place on the impious Elymas when the
apostle was 'filled with the Holy Ghost' (verse 9). The
resultant blindness of the sorcerer was due to 'the hand of the
Lord' being upon him (verse 11). Very instructive is Acts
xvi. 6–10, for here we see the Holy Spirit forbidding the
preachers to go to certain places, and directing them through
a dream to the place of His choice. Everywhere there is the
thought that the extension of the Church was to take place
and was taking place in accordance with the divine plan, not
as human skill or wisdom might direct. It was when the
Church walked 'in the fear of the Lord and in the comfort of
the Holy Ghost' that it 'was multiplied' (Acts ix. 31).

And the story has been repeated throughout the history of
the Church. In many places people are becoming used to
hearing Billy Graham say, with reference to the multitudes
who decide for Christ at his preaching, 'This is not my doing.
It is a work of the Holy Spirit.' Again and again missionaries
return to us from the scenes of their labours, and when they
have mighty advances to recount, say, 'Hear what the Spirit
of the Lord has been doing'. Never do they say, 'Listen to the
tale of how I won many people for God'. Those who are
most concerned with the advance of the Church are most
conscious of the fact that there is nothing of man in the
essential part of the process.

We see the same thing essentially in revivals which come
from time to time to the Church of God. Then the Holy
Spirit does a new thing. He shatters men's complacency, and
brings life where before all was dead. Men and women are
deeply stirred. Sinners are converted. Nominal Christians are
shaken out of their formalism and brought into genuine
experience of the Spirit's power. Those who are truly the
saints of God find their spiritual lives deepened. Often there is
something on the human level which helps to explain all this.
We can point, perhaps, to praying Christians, or to outstanding preaching, or to men living sanctified lives which
bear eloquent testimony to the divine power. But, important

as these things undoubtedly are, none of them is the really significant thing. That is the work of the Spirit. He, and He alone, can revive the Church. God chooses men to be His instruments. But that is the point. They are His *instruments*. They are no more than that. The effective work is His alone

CHAPTER VI

THE SPIRIT IN THE LIFE OF THE BELIEVER

BISHOP BUTLER concluded his interview with John Wesley by saying, 'Sir, this pretending to extraordinary revelation and gifts of the Holy Ghost is a horrid thing—a very horrid thing'.[1] Not many Christians today would, I think, be prepared to go all the way with the good bishop, but there are many for whom the idea of personal contact with the Holy Spirit is preposterous, and even vaguely embarrassing. They do not deny that there is such a thing as the gift of the Holy Spirit. But they seem to hold that it is an optional extra for honours students, so to speak. Outstanding saints may be inspired by the Holy Spirit, but hardly the rank and file of Church membership.

That is emphatically not the position of the New Testament. There the possession of the Spirit is the distinguishing mark of the believer. We have already noticed some Pauline passages bearing on the matter, as when that apostle said that if anybody lacks the Spirit he does not belong to Christ (Rom. viii. 9), whereas, conversely, if he is one of the sons of God he will be led by the Spirit (Rom. viii. 14).[2] Examples could be multiplied. There is a very interesting instance in Ephesians i. 13, where we read, 'having also believed, ye were sealed with the Holy Spirit of promise' (see also Eph. iv. 30). Sealing was a common custom in days when most men were illiterate. They could not read a label, but they could discern a distinguishing mark. Accordingly owners of property would often have a seal made to give a distinctive impression, an animal, say, or a particular geometric design. When this was stamped on an article it gave evidence of ownership. Everyone who saw the deer or the triangle (or whatever it

---

[1] M. W. Patterson, *A History of the Church of England*, London, 1912, p. 394.

[2] See above p. 37.

was) would know immediately, 'This belongs to old so-and-so.' In similar fashion the Holy Spirit within a man is the evidence that he belongs to God. The Holy Spirit is God's mark of ownership set upon him. The inference is inescapable. If we are God's, we will bear God's mark. His Holy Spirit will be within us.

The passages in Ephesians view the Spirit as the mark whereby people outside us may know that we are God's. The Spirit effects a transformation and we are seen to belong to Him. John has another thought. The Spirit within us is the evidence whereby we know that God wills to abide with His people. 'Hereby we know that he abideth in us, by the Spirit which he gave us' (1 Jn. iii. 24). And again, for this truth is important, 'hereby know we that we abide in him, and he in us, because he hath given us of his Spirit' (1 Jn. iv. 13). The believer is not left to work out the probabilities on the basis of his own best theological insights. He perceives in his own life evidences of a power not his own. He knows that the Holy Spirit is within him. And knowing this, he knows that God dwells among His people. The Spirit gives assurance. The Spirit gives an inner certainty.

THE SPIRIT'S REGENERATING WORK

All this might be held to be a conclusion from the premise that, as the Christian understands it, spiritual life is not a natural achievement, but the result of an activity of the Holy Spirit. By nature we are 'dead through (our) trespasses and sins' (Eph. ii. 1). 'The mind of the flesh is death' (Rom. viii. 6). There is no point in bidding a physically dead man get up and live. Shout as you will, he will not hear. And there is a similar phenomenon in the realm of the spirit. We would not even begin to be Christians without some work of the Spirit within us. The natural man likes to think that his salvation stems from his own strong right arm. The cross teaches us that this is not so. We are saved only by Christ's atoning death. But when we learn this we still tend to grasp at what we can. At least, we think, we may claim the credit for having

chosen Christ, for having turned from the world and cast in
our lot with the people of God. Not a bit of it, says the
Scripture. Left to ourselves, we would not wish to make even
the motion of turning from sin. We would simply stay
where we are. Every preacher of the gospel knows that his
principal difficulty is that he is proclaiming a wonderful way
of salvation to men who do not particularly want to be saved.
It is not until the Spirit of God begins to work in their hearts
that men are stirred enough to accept the gospel offer that is
made to them.

The very preaching of the gospel is done by or in the Holy
Spirit (1 Pet. i. 12), and its content is something that is
revealed by the same Spirit (Eph. iii. 5). When men are convicted of their sin, that is a work of the Spirit (Jn. xvi. 8f.).
We sometimes go astray here, and think of powerful preaching as the means whereby men are convicted. Preaching may
be the means the Spirit uses, but it is always the work of the
Spirit to convict men. If the Spirit does not convict, then
nothing that man can do can bring about that result. We have
a responsibility. We ought not to skimp in our work of
preparation or of delivering our messages. But we ought not
to trust in them either. Basically the deep-seated work that
goes on in men's hearts when they are awakened to their
sinfulness is the work of God's Spirit, not of human preachers.

Other Scriptures point to this basic truth, though without
express mention of the Spirit. Thus Lydia's heart was opened
(Acts xvi. 14). A veil must be taken from the heart before men
turn to the Lord (2 Cor. iii. 12-18). 'The word of the cross
is to them that are perishing foolishness' (1 Cor. i. 18). The
plain truth is that 'the natural man receiveth not the things of
the Spirit of God'. To him they are no more than 'foolishness'
(1 Cor. ii. 14). Only as a work of the Spirit is done in him can
the situation be any different.

But the Spirit does not simply convict men and leave it
at that. He brings life; He can be called 'the Spirit of life'
(Rom. viii. 2); He 'quickens' men (Jn. vi. 63; Rom. viii. 11).
H. J. Wotherspoon trenchantly says, 'Nothing was added to
the Church by Pentecost—no new truth, no new institution

nothing of apparatus; but only life itself.'[1] In our opening chapter we noticed a number of references to being 'born again', an activity ascribed to the Spirit (Jn. iii. 3, 5, 7). The Christian life is begun in the Spirit (Gal. iii. 3). Men are saved, 'not by works done in righteousness . . . but according to his mercy . . . through the washing of regeneration and renewing of the Holy Ghost' (Tit. iii. 5). The Spirit is joined with the Lord Jesus Christ in the activity of 'washing' believers (1 Cor. vi. 11). Christians can say 'in one Spirit were we all baptized into one body . . . and were all made to drink of one Spirit' (1 Cor. xii. 13; Goodspeed translates the latter section as 'we have all been saturated with one Spirit').

There are other ways of putting it. Our list is not exhaustive. Now this great variety of forms of expression points impressively to one great central truth, namely, that the Christian life is due to supernatural action. Christianity does not simply mean a moral change within men. It is more than merely 'turning over a new leaf'. It is such a radical change that the man can be said to have been born all over again. He can be said to be created anew (2 Cor. v. 17). This is not anything that men may do for themselves. It takes place as a result of the work of the Spirit of God. We cannot begin to understand what Christianity is all about until we have grasped this.

GOD'S DWELLING WITH MAN

In all this we are not to think of a passing contact with the Divine as though the Spirit induced life within the believer and then politely took His leave. There is a permanent union. The Holy Spirit 'dwelleth in us' (2 Tim. i. 14; 'dwelleth' conveys the idea of someone living in a house!). The Spirit takes up residence in the believer. The same idea is put in a slightly different form in the passages we have already considered in another connection, where first the Church and then the believer's body are said to be the 'temple of the Holy Ghost' (1 Cor. iii. 16, vi. 19). There is something solid and

---

[1] *What Happened at Pentecost?* Edinburgh, 1937, p. 26.

substantial and lasting about a temple. And when the Holy Ghost is thought of as dwelling within us as in a temple, there is the thought that He has not come as it were in passing, but that He has chosen to make His habitation with us. Similarly in Ephesians ii. 21f. we read of 'a holy temple in the Lord', in which believers are 'builded together for a habitation of God in the Spirit'. Here the word 'habitation' conveys the notion of 'settling down'. Again there is the thought of permanence.

The Christian life, then, is a life of continual communion with God. It does not mean that God vouchsafes us an occasional fleeting glimpse of Himself. He takes up His abode with us and in us. The Christian is never separated from the indwelling presence of the Holy Spirit. This, I think, is not only a way of saying that God is always with us to supply us with whatever we need. It surely means that God delights to dwell with us for the purpose of fellowship. It means that day by day we may know intimate communion with that Friend who 'sticketh closer than a brother'.

There is a very lovely reference in the first chapter of Philippians. Here the apostle Paul is contemplating the possibility of his dying a martyr's death (verse 20). Even in the face of this last extremity he looks for 'the supply of the Spirit of Jesus Christ' (verse 19). From the first stirrings of spiritual life until the end of his days the Christian must look to the Spirit of God.

This truth has not always been realized by the Christian Church. Thus Swete, rejecting Hort's idea that Acts ix. 31 is to be understood of an invocation of the Holy Spirit, points out that 'the attitude of the primitive Church towards the Spirit was rather one of joyful welcome than of invocation; the cry *Veni, Creator Spiritus* belongs to a later age, when the Spirit was sought and perhaps expected, but not regarded as a Guest Who had already come, and come to abide'.[1] The permanent indwelling of the Spirit is a very precious part of the Christian faith.

[1] *The Holy Spirit in the New Testament*, London, 1910, p. 96, n.2.

THE FREEDOM OF THE SPIRIT

'Where the Spirit of the Lord is, there is liberty' writes Paul (2 Cor. iii. 17), and the words are the charter of Christian freedom. Christianity is not a device for hedging men about with all manner of restrictions. Nor is the Christian unable to move without the *nihil obstat* of some repressive external authority. He has been born into (or adopted into, if you prefer the imagery of Rom. viii. 15f. and Gal. iv. 5f.) the glorious liberty of the sons of God. Other religions may press men down with a multitude of burdensome requirements. Other religions may interpose an indispensable hierarchy between the seeking soul and God. But Christianity introduces us to a sphere where all is of grace not law (did not Augustine say 'Love God and do what you like'?), a sphere where even the humblest believer has the right of immediate access to the very presence of God Himself (Heb. x. 19). The Spirit of God is within him. The Spirit of God informs and guides him. And where the Spirit is, there is freedom from pressing restraints.

This does not mean that the Christian is subject to no law of any kind. Liberty is not license. As R. H. Strachan says, 'Christian freedom is not the abolition of all constraint. It is the acceptance of a new constraint, which operates not from without, but from within. It is *open freedom*, not enforced, but free acceptance of the will of God (cf. John viii. 31ff.). It is the end of legal religion.'[1] The Christian feels himself subject indeed to the law of God. But this is a matter of inner conviction as well as of the Word of God. The Spirit of God within him works the necessary changes. As far as outward things are concerned he is completely free.

One freedom which is specifically mentioned is that of access to the heavenly Father: 'through him (i.e. Christ) we both have our access in one Spirit unto the Father' (Eph. ii. 18). The word rendered 'access' is thought by some to be

---

[1] *Moffatt Commentary, in loc.* Cf. also A. Plummer, 'Service voluntarily rendered to Him who is the Truth is the most perfect freedom of which a creature is capable' (*I.C.C., in loc.*).

better understood as 'introduction'. Whether this be so or not, the important point is that the individual believer is brought into the very presence of the Father through the activity of the Spirit. Not for him the laborious approach through dead works. Not for him the elaborate ritual of sacrifice. He has been adopted into the heavenly family, and he approaches the heavenly Father through the Spirit.

'The law of the Spirit of life in Christ Jesus made me free from the law of sin and of death' writes Paul (Rom. viii. 2). Primarily these words refer to law as a way of salvation, but we may consider them to point to a liberty that pervades the whole of life. We do not speak much these days of bondage to law. But what of our attitude to convention? 'Think of the extent to which our own Christian faith and practice, our grasp of what Christianity really means, and our power to put that into practical experiment, are limited, restricted, by the pressure of all those subtle and powerful influences which our environment exerts upon us, the influence of our home, our set, our business, of public opinion in our neighbourhood, even of our church.'[1] The circumstances of life have a cramping effect on most of us. But the living God brings those who receive His Holy Spirit out into a place of large horizons.

POWER THROUGH THE SPIRIT

One of Paul's favourite preaching points (if we may judge by the way in which he mentions it in his Epistles) was the contrast between mere words and the power which the gospel brings into men's lives. Thus he reminds the Corinthians that his preaching in their city was 'not in persuasive words of wisdom, but in demonstration of the Spirit and of power: that your faith should not stand in the wisdom of men, but in the power of God' (1 Cor. ii. 4f.). For him it was a matter of prime importance that he did not come merely telling men what they ought to do. He came telling them of a power by which they could do it.

[1] F. A. Cockin, *The Holy Spirit and the Church*, London, 1939, p. 85.

A missionary has told me of a poster which evidently had quite a vogue in China in an earlier day. It depicts a man in a muddy pit. A representative of Confucianism sees him there and tells him that if he had followed the teachings of Confucius he would not be in his present plight. But the man is still in the pit. A Buddhist comes along with the good advice that if ever he gets out he must walk in the ways of Buddha and he will never fall in again. But the man is still in the pit. Then the Christian comes along and throws down a rope and pulls him out. In this pictorial form is demonstrated the truth that there is much of ethical value in the various religions of the world. If men lived up to the highest and best such religions teach, they would not be caught in the pit of sin. But they *are* in the pit of sin. And such faiths are powerless to pull them out. The distinctive thing about the Christian view of the Spirit is that the infinite divine resources of God Himself are available for the humblest believer, to enable him to live the Christian life. The Christian is 'daily breathed upon by an invisible Power of good'.[1]

Our Lord Himself knew the same power, for 'God anointed him with the Holy Ghost and with power' (Acts x. 38). He told His followers that they would receive power when the Holy Spirit came upon them (Acts i. 8). In the same way, Paul speaks of the gospel as being 'not . . . in word only, but also in power, and in the Holy Ghost' (1 Thes. i. 5). The note of power runs through the New Testament, as it must through the experience of every true child of God.

I like the story of the drunkard who was converted, and who later came across some of his mates. On hearing what had happened they were amused, and somewhat cynical. 'You don't mean to tell me that you believe the Bible!' said one of them. 'Do you really think that Jesus changed water into wine?' 'Well, I don't know about that,' came the reply. 'But I do know that in my house He has changed beer into furniture!' And in its measure the same is true of everyone who has come to a saving knowledge of Christ. When Christ

[1] From a letter of Professor Hort, cited by F. W. Beare, *The Firs Epistle of Peter*, Oxford, 1947, p. 53.

comes into a man's life, so does His Holy Spirit. The Spirit comes with creative power, and in the power of the Spirit that man is able to do things he could never do before. The Spirit does not simply tell men what to do; He gives them strength to do it.

This does not mean, as some hold, that the Christian is passive, that he sits back, so to speak, and lets the Spirit of God do all the work. The New Testament does not inculcate a negative attitude. It has injunctions like 'fight the good fight' (1 Tim. vi. 12), 'even so run, that ye may attain' (1 Cor. ix. 24; verse 25 speaks of 'striving' for an incorruptible crown), 'let us cleanse ourselves' (2 Cor. vii. 1), 'bear ye one another's burdens' (Gal. vi. 2), 'be strong in the Lord. . . . Put on the whole armour of God, that ye may be able to stand against the wiles of the devil. For our wrestling is not against flesh and blood . . .' (Eph. vi. 10ff.), 'mortify therefore your members' (Col. iii. 5), and many others. The list could be prolonged indefinitely. There is not the slightest doubt that the New Testament requires vigorous effort on the part of the believer. But the point is that this effort is to be made in the strength of the divine Spirit, not in the energy of the flesh. The position is made clear in Philippians ii. 12f.: 'work out your own salvation with fear and trembling; for it is God which worketh in you both to will and to work. . . .' Edwin H. Palmer cites this passage and comments, 'If we work without the Spirit, we will be frustrated. On the other hand, if we leave it all to the Spirit and do not work, we will also end in failure. But combine the Spirit with work, then increasing victory will be ours. The secret of holy living is found in this combination'.[1]

GUIDANCE

One of the perplexing things in life is knowing what is the right line to take in a difficult situation. Everyone knows the problem of being at one's wits' end, and yet having to do something. Here the Christian has a wonderful promise from

[1] *The Holy Spirit*, Grand Rapids, 1958, p. 97.

the Master Himself: 'when he, the Spirit of truth, is come, he shall guide you into all the truth' (Jn. xvi. 13). This gives a general charter which we may claim in all sorts of situations. We should probably understand 1 John ii. 20 in the same way: 'ye have an anointing from the Holy One, and ye all know' (RV mg.). Some religious groups in antiquity, e.g. the Gnostics, laid claim to secret knowledge known only to a select group. 'John points out that there is no such select group in Christianity, for God gives His Holy Spirit to all believers, and they all have knowledge.'[1] There is a specific promise also for times of facing hostile tribunals: 'be not anxious beforehand what ye shall speak: but whatsoever shall be given you in that hour, that speak ye: for it is not ye that speak, but the Holy Ghost' (Mk. xiii. 11).

Later in the New Testament we find Christians acting in accordance with promises like these. In Acts ii. 4 they spoke as the Spirit enabled them. In Acts xv. 28 they can say, concerning the solution of a difficult problem, 'it seemed good to the Holy Ghost, and to us'. In Acts xvi. 6ff. we see them being guided by the Spirit to go and preach in the right place. And these experiences have been repeated by Christian men and women through the centuries. The Spirit does guide us. He does show us the way in which we should go. He does give the words that are necessary when we need His help.

Archbishop William Temple once said that he often had the experience of calling on people with no reason other than an inner leading, and finding that he was able to render them significant spiritual help. But, he added, when his spiritual life was not right, when he had in some degree slipped away from close fellowship with God, these occasions became much rarer.

This experience can be paralleled by many a Christian worker. When we really are living close to God we know the reality of the Spirit's guiding. When our spiritual life grows dim we do not appreciate His guidance so much. It is not, I think, that He ceases to guide. Rather we cease to be in a condition to apprehend His guidance. But the guidance is

[1] *The New Bible Commentary*, London, 1954, p. 1154 (on 1 Jn. ii. 20).

very real. There is the alternative danger of interpreting our own feelings and opinions as the Spirit's guidance. Our best defence against this temptation is a real humility joined with a genuine readiness to hear and obey the Spirit. If we are sincerely seeking to know God's will, and are ready to follow it, wherever it may lead, then His guidance will certainly be afforded us.

Of particular importance is the revelation that the Spirit has made. There are 'things which eye saw not, and ear heard not, and which entered not into the heart of man'. But Paul can add, 'But unto us God revealed them through the Spirit' (1 Cor. ii. 9f.). In other words, the gospel is not devised by man's best thought. It is something that man would never have guessed at. If he is ever to learn it, it will have to be told to him. And it *has* been told to him! It has been revealed to him by none less than the very Spirit of God Himself.

The Spirit did this in the exercise of His sovereign freedom. From Ephesians iii. 5 we find that the gospel 'in other generations was not made known unto the sons of men, as it hath now been revealed unto his holy apostles and prophets in the Spirit'. In other words, the revelation did not come when men wanted it, but when God willed that it should be given. The revelation is not at man's command; it comes as and when the Spirit wills.

In other days the revelation was made directly to the apostles and prophets, but for us it is found in the Bible. The Spirit is regarded as the Author of the Bible.[1] Therefore we will chiefly look to Scripture to guide us on our way. There are references to the Spirit as 'speaking' (e.g. Acts xxi. 11; 1 Tim. iv. 1) so that we may well feel that the Spirit within the believer moves him, and applies the basic revelation to the needs of the day. But we will not look to some extraordinary disturbance within ourselves as the usual mode of guidance. Rather we will expect that the Bible will provide us with the great principles that we need. 'Men spake from God, being moved by the Holy Ghost' (2 Pet. i. 21). And the Spirit-inspired Book will be the chief means of affording us guidance.

[1] See above. pp. 50f.

CHAPTER VII

THE FRUIT OF THE SPIRIT

IN our chapter on the Spirit in the Old Testament we
noticed the view common in antiquity that the presence
of a divine spirit would be shown by a frenzy or the like.
Madness, unpredictability, convulsive physical movements
and similar phenomena presented irrefutable evidence to men
of those days that a divine spirit had taken possession of a man.
Such views were as widely current in the world of the New
Testament as of the Old. Frenzied ravings were the stock-in-
trade of the prophets in more than one religion. And even
where the worst excesses of this type were eschewed, the
tendency was to detect the divine in the unusual, in pre-
dictions of the future, in special insight, in a penetrating
knowledge of the hearts of men.

Against such a background it is profoundly important to
notice that the New Testament puts its emphasis where the
Old Testament showed the way—on the moral and ethical
results of the Spirit's indwelling. The New Testament knows
of prophets who can predict the future. It does not overlook
the enormous practical importance of divine guidance. It
affords examples of Spirit-filled men with unusual powers of
insight. But again and again it comes back to the point that
when the Holy Spirit of God comes into a man, that man lives
on a higher ethical plane. The popular emphasis on the
spectacular and the inexplicable has given way to an emphasis
on solid Christian character. This is not mere moralism. It
rests on and lays stress on the supernatural. But the supernatural work of the Spirit is made manifest in moral uprightness.

THE FLESH AND THE SPIRIT

This is sometimes brought out by contrasting life 'in the flesh'
with that 'in the Spirit' (see especially Rom. viii. 1-14;

Gal. v. 16–26). 'Flesh', of course, denotes properly an important constituent of the body. The New Testament often uses
the word in this way, for example, in the expression 'flesh
and blood'. From this it comes to mean that which is simply
outward and visible. The word can be used to denote life in
the body. By a natural development it comes to signify
imperfection, as when man in the flesh is set over against God,
or when this life is contrasted with that to come. It is not a long
step from that to thinking of the flesh as the lower part of
man's nature, and thus as especially linked with sin. The term
may thus have an ethical content. In view of this variety of
meaning, New Testament passages containing the word must
be studied carefully. Sometimes it is used without any sense
of blame. At others there is the definite note of concern as the
lusting of man's lower passions is implied.

Our immediate business is with the contrast sometimes
made between flesh and spirit. This may be a contrast between
two parts of man's nature, between his higher self and his
lower self. But when a Christian begins to think of his higher
self, he begins to think about the Holy Spirit of God. He
knows full well that anything that is good in him is owing to
God. When he thinks of the force making for righteousness
within his being, he thinks not of his own best effort, but of
the Holy Spirit of God. Thus even though 'spirit' be spelled
with a small 's' and denote the spirit of man, the thought of the
Holy Spirit is not far away, and the New Testament writers
pass insensibly from one to the other.

The references to life in the flesh remind us that there are
standards of conduct which appeal to the natural man. He has
desires which do not accord with the dictates of the Spirit of
God. Indeed, part of the work of the Spirit is to show up
every evil within man. 'The more sanctified a man is, the more
will he acknowledge the wretchedness of his own heart. This
is the saving work of the Holy Spirit: this is the deepening
conviction of sin without which no man shall be sanctified.'[1]
Sometimes desire issues in crude lust, which, I suppose, is

[1] E. F. Kevan, *The Saving Work of the Spirit*, London, 1953, p. 24.

what most people in modern times associate with 'the flesh'. But there are 'desires ... of the mind' which may be linked to 'desires of the flesh' (Eph. ii. 3). Personal fastidiousness may cause a man to forswear all blatant forms of lust, and yet he may be living 'according to the flesh' in the New Testament understanding of it. The flesh, in short, stands for that part of man's nature wherein his natural desires have free rein. 'I know that in *me*,' writes Paul, 'that is, in *my flesh*, dwelleth no good thing' (Rom. vii. 18). The flesh is the whole man, apart from Christ. Life 'in the flesh', then, may issue in a repulsive pandering to the more obvious forms of self-gratification. Or it may result, if the flesh is very 'nice' flesh, in a refined, artistic or intellectual pursuit of one's aims and desires. It may even take on a religious hue, though the religion will perforce be that acceptable to man, and not subject to uncomfortable demands on the part of God. The characteristic thing is bondage to one's human nature rather than submission to the Spirit of God.

Somewhere I recall reading of a young husband whose marriage was on the point of breaking up. His wife had announced her determination to leave him for another man. In his extremity he sought out his minister, and asked his aid. The clergyman called upon the wife and tried to reason with her. She heard him out, and then said, 'Nothing that you can say will shake my determination. I no longer love my husband. Life with him would be inexpressibly dreary. I have a right to be happy, and I mean to claim that right.' Those words, 'I have a right to be happy', perfectly express the mind of the flesh. No matter at what cost to others, no matter at what ultimate cost to himself, the fleshly person claims the right to be happy. All other considerations must be subordinate to that.

What such an attitude can lead to is made clear by the dreadful catalogue of 'works of the flesh' in Galatians v. 19-21. The sexual uncleanness, the self-assertion, the self-indulgence and all the rest arise from the basic determination to pursue the path of one's own pleasures without regard to anything else. The flesh 'lusteth against the Spirit, and the Spirit against the flesh; for these are contrary the one to the other' (Gal. v. 17).

The fleshly nature is concerned with the self. The Spirit is concerned with wider responsibilities, and especially with the glory of God. Inevitably the two are implacably opposed. As Paul says simply, 'they that are after the flesh do mind the things of the flesh; but they that are after the spirit the things of the spirit' (Rom. viii. 5), and he goes on to remind us that 'the mind of the flesh is death . . . the mind of the flesh is enmity against God . . . they that are in the flesh cannot please God' (Rom. viii. 6–8). Logically, inevitably, 'if ye live after the flesh, ye must die' (Rom. viii. 13).

But Christians are not shut up to these grim possibilities. Of them Paul goes on to say, 'ye are not in the flesh, but in the spirit, if so be that the Spirit of God dwelleth in you' (Rom. viii. 9). The last word is not with the flesh but with the Spirit of God.

SANCTIFICATION

Sometimes this work of the Spirit is spoken of in terms of sanctification. Christians are 'elect . . . according to the fore-knowledge of God the Father, in sanctification of the Spirit' (1 Pet. i. 1f.). God chose them 'from the beginning unto salvation in sanctification of the Spirit' (2 Thes. ii. 13).

The essential idea in sanctification is that of being made holy. That, in turn, brings up the question of the meaning of 'holy'. In the Bible it is always the quality of being set apart for God, in whom alone true holiness is found. But those who are set apart for God must partake of the qualities of character that are appropriate to such a state. Sanctification may thus refer to the being set apart for God, or to the growth in Christian graces that is a necessary part of the Christian life.

In one sense sanctification may be regarded as already completed. Paul tells the Corinthians 'ye were sanctified' (1 Cor. vi. 11), where the aorist tense points to an act done once and for all. Similarly in Ephesians v. 26 we are told that Christ gave Himself up for the Church, 'that he might sanctify it'. Again there is an aorist, which points to the sanctification in question as being effected at the cross. It may be that the occasional linking of the Spirit with justification points to something of the same kind (1 Cor. vi. 11). At any rate it associates the Spirit with the beginning of the specifically Christian life.

This idea that sanctification is in some sense already effected will bear close attention. There are some who understand it to mean that sanctification is an activity of the Spirit completely separate from justification, and completed in a moment. Conversion and rebirth come as one spiritual crisis, and sanctification as altogether another.

But sanctification is not to be separated in this way from the beginning of spiritual life. The justified believer is also in principle sanctified. We can deduce no less from the activity of the Spirit within him as he passes from death into life. And that is what this past sanctification points us to. The basic idea in sanctification is that of being set apart for God, of belonging to Him. All believers (and not only the outstandingly good) are spoken of in the New Testament as 'saints', i.e. as men set apart for God. We have been set apart to be God's own, else we are none of His. In this sense our sanctification has already taken place.

But sanctification is not exhausted by this initial experience. From another point of view sanctification is the continuing process whereby the believer grows in the things of God. It is a progressive increase in holiness. Begun at conversion, it is never finished till the day we complete our earthly pilgrimage. Thus the Corinthians are urged to cleanse themselves from 'all defilement of flesh and spirit, perfecting holiness in the fear of God' (2 Cor. vii. 1). The fact that holiness can be 'perfected' shows that it is progressive in its nature. Throughout the whole of our lives we are engaged in an activity of defeating sin, and producing righteousness. And this is done, and can be done, only in the strength of the Holy Spirit. It is 'by the spirit' that we 'mortify the deeds of the body' (Rom. viii. 13). The kingdom of God is 'righteousness and peace and joy', not in themselves, but 'in the Holy Ghost' (Rom. xiv. 17). The Christian is transformed by the activity of the Spirit of the Lord.

POSITIVE VIRTUES

The Spirit's work in overcoming our lower nature, and leading us away from sin, is not merely a negative thing. We have already noticed more than one way of bringing out its positive force. One of special appeal is that of referring to 'the fruit of the Spirit'. 'The fruit of the Spirit', Paul tells us, 'is love, joy, peace, longsuffering, kindness, goodness, faithfulness, meekness, temperance (or self-control)' (Gal. v. 22f.). It may not be without significance that 'fruit' is in the singular. Paul is thinking of these qualities of character as a single cluster, so that every Christian should experience them all. It is not that one Christian gives evidence of love, another of joy, and so on. All Christians are expected to manifest all of these qualities. This would be a tall order, indeed, were it not that this fruit is 'of the Spirit'. Because the very power of God is operative within the lives of Christian people they are able to produce fruit that else would be completely beyond them.

Especially is love connected with the Spirit. Paul can appeal to 'the love of the Spirit' (Rom. xv. 30) as a motive for the prayers of the Romans. The Spirit had produced the bond that united Paul to the Christians of the city that he had never seen. Again, Epaphras told Paul of the Colossians' 'love in the Spirit' (Col. i. 8), another church that Paul had never visited. In the same way Paul thinks of 'the love of God' as being 'shed abroad in our hearts through the Holy Ghost which was given unto us' (Rom. v. 5; Moffatt renders, 'God's love floods our hearts through the holy Spirit . . .'). The imagery is like that of Isaiah xliv. 3f. Through the Spirit's action the love of God is poured without stint into our dry and barren hearts like floods of water on to drought-parched soil.

The Christian idea of love is different from that which we see elsewhere. It is a quality of love which recks not of merit in the beloved. It is seen in the cross of Christ, where the Son of God laid down His perfect life for men who were sinners (Rom. v. 8). Sinners; those whom God hates (Ps. v. 5). In other words, Christ died for men in whom there was nothing attractive. They are described in Scripture as 'foolish, disobedient, deceived, serving divers lusts and pleasures, living in malice and envy, hateful, hating one another' (Tit. iii. 3). But in that situation 'the kindness of God our Saviour, and his love toward man, appeared' (verse 4). He loved them so greatly, not because sinners as such are attractive to God, but because it is God's nature to love. When we realize that the divine love is like that, and when we yield ourselves to the God who loves like that, then we are transformed by His love and His power. We begin to see men in a measure as God sees them. We love, not because of merit in the sinners we meet, but because we, too, are coming to love because of our inmost nature. And that is something that men, left to themselves, never accomplish. It is not a human possibility. It is a work of the Holy Spirit. He pours into our hearts a love of which we are completely incapable out of our own resources. He suffuses our lives with a 'love divine, all loves excelling'.

Righteousness is often connected with the Spirit. The kingdom of God, Paul tells us, is 'righteousness and peace and joy in the Holy Ghost' (Rom. xiv. 17). Men know what righteousness is. They know that they ought to live righteously. The trouble is that approving the better, they do the worse. But the man in whom the Spirit is is not limited in this fashion. For him there is a new power, and a power that overflows into righteous living. The righteousness that was for ever unattainable, as long as he lived in his own strength, is now a blessed reality, thanks to the Spirit of God within him.

Notice that 'peace and joy' are linked with righteousness in the passage to which we have just referred. Peace with us is merely negative. It signifies the absence of war or strife. But among the Hebrews of old, and among the men of the New Testament, it was a term with a very positive meaning. Peace for them denoted the prosperity of the whole man, and particularly spiritual prosperity. Man's basic problem is his alienation from God. His sin makes him the enemy of God (Col. i. 21). But in Christ Jesus the believer finds his sin put away. The enmity between him and God is bridged over. He is reconciled. He is at peace with God. And when a man is at peace with God then he has a deep-seated peace that nothing on earth can shake. In other words he has entered that state for which God created him. He has that prosperity, in the widest sense, that matters most of all. And that, too, is a gift of the Holy Spirit.

With it Paul links joy, and, indeed, joy is often linked with the Spirit. On one occasion our Lord 'rejoiced in the Holy Spirit' (Lk. x. 21; Weymouth translates, 'was filled by the Holy Spirit with rapturous joy'). When the Spirit came upon the disciples on the day of Pentecost they were accused of being full of new wine. Evidently the experience made them merry, even hilarious. Even in a time of persecution 'the disciples were filled with joy and with the Holy Ghost' (Acts xiii. 52; cf. 1 Thes. i. 6). Joy is part of the fruit of the Spirit (Gal. v. 22). The word for joy and its derivatives (like grace, one of the words for forgiveness, etc.) occur with startling frequency in the pages of the Greek New Testament. The early Christians were for the most part members of the depressed classes, slaves, women, and the like. They had little enough to rejoice about if they confined their attention to their outward circumstances. But they did not confine their attention to their earthly circumstances; they rose above them. The Holy Spirit of God put a deep and abiding joy into their hearts. Nothing in the world could give such a joy. And nothing in the world could take it away. It is a curious fact to one who is deeply read in the New Testament that in modern times Christians are so often accused of being killjoys. One would never gather this from the New Testament. If men have no joy, they do not have the religion of the New Testament. Joy is one of the Spirit's good gifts to men. And as we yield to the Spirit's leadings we shall certainly find the joy of the Lord.

The story could be continued. The gifts of the Spirit are manifold, and the life of him in whom the Spirit dwells is wonderfully enriched. Enough, I think, has been said to make that clear. Christ did not come to impoverish life, but to bring the abundant life, and that life is lived through His Spirit.

CHAPTER VIII

THE FULLNESS OF THE SPIRIT

THERE are several examples in the New Testament of men and women who are said to be 'filled' with the Holy Spirit. This was the case with John the Baptist from his mother's womb (Lk. i. 15), evidently a permanent condition. Rather different are the statements that both his parents were filled with the Spirit (Lk. i. 41, 67), for in both cases what is meant is a sudden burst of inspiration. These are probably all examples of the working of the Spirit in the Old Testament sense rather than in that of the New Testament.

Our Lord Himself was filled with the Spirit (Lk. iv. 1), and after His ministry a number of His followers had the same experience, as Peter (Acts iv. 8), Stephen (Acts vi. 5, vii. 55), Saul (Acts ix. 17, xiii. 9), and Barnabas (Acts xi. 24). In addition to these outstanding people there are several instances where a number of people, such as the Seven (Acts vi. 3), or the whole group of believers on a particular occasion (Acts ii. 4, iv. 31, xiii. 52), are said to be filled with the Spirit. Clearly this phenomenon was expected to take place widely. Outstanding leaders should be conspicuous for it, but then, so should ordinary believers. Sometimes there is the thought of a permanent endowment (Acts vi. 5, ix. 17, xi. 24), sometimes the thought of a particular gift for a special occasion (Acts iv. 8, xiii. 9).

Outside the Lucan writings it does not appear that anyone is actually said to be filled with the Spirit. There is an injunction in Ephesians v. 18, translated as 'be filled with the Spirit'. If this is the correct understanding of it, Christians in general are commanded to experience the fullness of the Spirit. But the Greek construction is not that for being filled 'with' anything. It denotes being filled either 'in' or 'by'. As Griffith Thomas says, it 'indicates that the Spirit is the Sphere in which, or the Agent by Whom, not the Person or Matter of

Whom, we are filled'.[1] If the Spirit be the Spirit of God, the meaning is 'be filled in the sphere of the Spirit' or 'make sure that it is the Spirit who performs the act of filling you'. Many expositors, however, believe that it is the spirit of the believer, and not the Spirit of God, that is meant, the meaning being, 'be filled in (your) spirit', i.e. 'let your highest faculty, not your lowest, be richly supplied with that which you crave, so that its especial powers are called into play'.[2] Even if this be the understanding of it, however, there is agreement that this can be done only in the strength which the Holy Spirit supplies, so it amounts to the same thing. However the linguistic problem be resolved, the duty is laid upon us of seeing that we receive in full measure the filling that only the Spirit of God can bring. But, whatever our understanding of this passage, it is impossible to deny that the New Testament as a whole envisages that all believers will experience in the fullest measure the indwelling and the enriching of the Holy Spirit.

Notice that Paul puts this injunction in close connection with another, 'be not drunken with wine'. The fullness of the Spirit is accompanied by a holy exhilaration, so that those on whom the Spirit came at Pentecost were accused of being drunken (Acts ii. 13). The Spirit-filled life is not a sad and staid affair. While the Spirit-filled man is the possessor of a deep and abiding peace, he is also a man aflame. John Mackay reminds us of J. R. Seeley's dictum, 'No soul is pure that is not passionate, no virtue is safe that is not enthusiastic'.[3] He ascribes much of Communism's success to the fact that it is 'a singing faith',[4] and deplores the fact that the Church has all too often followed the line expressed in the inscription on a bell hung in the belfry of a Cambridge church, to protest against the work of Charles Simeon, 'Glory to the Church and damnation to enthusiasts'.[5] While there must be due order, and while fanaticism must be sharply discouraged, yet the Church of Jesus Christ will never accomplish its mission

---

[1] *The Holy Spirit of God*, London, 1913, p. 278.

[2] B. F. Westcott, *in loc*. He adds, 'It is assumed that the Spirit of God can alone satisfy the spirit of man.'

[3] *God's Order*, London, 1953, p. 217.   [4] P. 220.   [5] P. 221.

without the sheer joy of Jesus Christ. The fullness of the Spirit combines ardour and order. We should overlook neither.

Sometimes today Christians speak about being 'baptized' with the Holy Spirit. The New Testament references to this basically go back to the statement by John the Baptist that whereas he baptized with water, the One who came after him would baptize with the Holy Spirit (Mt. iii. 11; Mk. i. 8; Lk. iii. 16; Jn. i. 33). The risen Lord reiterated this, and pointed the disciples to the coming fulfilment (Acts i. 5). Finally Peter, when he was recounting the way the Holy Spirit fell on the believers in the house of Cornelius, said: 'And I remembered the word of the Lord, how that he said, John indeed baptized with water; but ye shall be baptized with the Holy Ghost' (Acts xi. 16).

The point about all these sayings is that they appear to look to the decisive outpouring of the Holy Spirit on the day of Pentecost. They are related to the gift of the Spirit at the beginning of the Church. The people in the house of Cornelius are an addition, but an addition that symbolizes that the gift is made available to Gentiles as to Jews. It is clear that Peter recognizes, in what took place in Cornelius' house, a fulfilment of the words of the Lord. There is no indication that they point to a continuing activity, repeated in the life of every believer. The baptism of the Spirit both in Acts ii and in Acts x was something striking and spectacular. It could be observed. It was accompanied by unusual phenomena in the way of 'speaking with tongues'.

There is, I think, but one passage which ascribes to all believers a baptism 'in the Spirit', namely, 1 Corinthians xii. 13: 'For in one Spirit were we all baptized into one body . . . and were all made to drink of one Spirit.' Here the emphasis is on the unity of all believers by virtue of this baptism. It is an experience in which all share, the apostle Paul and all the Corinthian believers, though some of these latter had made but little progress in the faith (Paul can speak of some of them as 'carnal', as 'babes in Christ', 1 Cor. iii. 1). The baptism in question obviously refers not to a supreme experience somewhere along the Christian way, but to the very beginning of

Christian experience. In the words of René Pache, it is 'the act whereby God gives to the believer his position in Jesus Christ. . . . All that we subsequently become and receive springs from that position in Christ, which the Spirit's baptism confers upon us'.[1] It may not be without significance that, though Christ is said to have been filled with the Spirit, He is not said to have been baptized with the Spirit. This baptism is the result of His work for men. Again, believers are never urged to seek the baptism of the Spirit, which is natural enough if they have already received this baptism at the beginning of their Christian life. Dr. Donald Grey Barnhouse says trenchantly, 'no one may ask a believer whether he has been baptized with the Spirit. The very fact that a man is *in* the body of Christ demonstrates that he has been baptized of the Spirit, for there is no other way of entering the body.'[2]

I do not wish to make a mountain out of the terminology. All that I am concerned to contend for is that we are better advised to think in terms of being 'filled' with the Spirit, than of being 'baptized' by the Spirit. The former points to an unspectacular, but very necessary happening, the gift of the Spirit in such wise as to transform the life of the believer. The latter might encourage the thought that there must be a spiritual crisis, with the Holy Spirit descending in some spectacular fashion. In practice it is often associated with the expectation of speaking in 'tongues'. Nothing of the sort is, of course, necessary. What is necessary is that we should learn that the life of the humblest believer may be filled with the Spirit.[3]

[1] *The Person and Work of the Holy Spirit*, London, 1956, p. 70.

[2] *The Keswick Week*, 1948 (London, 1948), p. 59. Cf. also W. H. Griffith Thomas: 'the view that the baptism of the Holy Ghost is a second distinct work of grace after conversion is without any warrant in Holy Scripture, especially as the phrase, "the baptism of the Holy Ghost", is not found in the New Testament' (*op. cit.*, p. 277).

[3] The subject is discussed at greater length by W. Graham Scroggie, in *The Baptism of the Spirit and Speaking with Tongues*, London, n.d., pp. 1–23. I cannot agree with all Dr. Scroggie says, more particularly with his refusal to see any reference to water baptism in certain passages, but his main argument, that the baptism of the Spirit is associated with Christian beginnings, is convincing.

THE GIFT OF GOD

How do men obtain the fullness of the Spirit? The New Testament repeats over and over that it is the gift of God. It does not come about as a result of our striving, or, indeed, of anything that we do. It comes as God's gift to us, or it does not come at all. God 'giveth his Holy Spirit unto you' (1 Thes. iv. 8).

But though it is a gift of God, it is not one that is given to all men indiscriminately. Some of God's gifts are like that, as, for example, those of which Barnabas and Paul spoke to the men of Lystra: 'he did good, and gave you from heaven rains and fruitful seasons, filling your hearts with food and gladness' (Acts xiv. 17). But the Spirit comes only to those who are ready to receive Him. The natural man 'receiveth not the things of the Spirit of God: for they are foolishness unto him; and he cannot know them, because they are spiritually judged' (1 Cor. ii. 14). That is to say, the man who is outside Christ, the man who lives a merely 'natural' life, with his own advantage as his main criterion, by that very fact cuts himself off from the good gift of the Spirit. To him the Christian, with his renunciation of the world, the flesh and the devil, is pursuing a meaningless path. The way of the cross does not make sense to him. And while he is in that state he cannot receive the Spirit. It is not that God, so to speak, deliberately withholds His gift. It is rather that the man simply cannot receive it. He has neither the inclination nor the capacity.

We must be clear on the point that we have a personal responsibility here. Though all Christians have the Spirit, not all have the fullness of the Spirit. The difference is the result of differing attitudes. Though the gift in one sense is all of God, in another sense it is up to us whether we are ready to receive it. As Edwin H. Palmer puts it, 'Man is 100 per cent responsible, and yet God gives man *all* of the ability that he has.'[1]

---

[1] *The Holy Spirit*, Grand Rapids, 1958, p. 173. Dr. Palmer states the divine side just as emphatically: 'the work of giving the Spirit rests entirely with God—100 per cent' (*ibid.*). He speaks of a paradoxical 'hundred-hundred' proposition, and not of a 'fifty-fifty' one.

Developing the former point he says: 'the responsibility rests 100 per cent on man. If he neglects the means that God has given, he will not have more of the Spirit. On the other hand, if he uses these means, he will have the Spirit in an increased measure. The obligation to seek this further indwelling of the Holy Spirit rests entirely with man.'[1]

The first point we shall notice by way of guidance in receiving the Spirit comes from the words of our Lord, who tells us that the heavenly Father gives the Spirit 'to them that ask him' (Lk. xi. 13). Again He gives the invitation to receive the Spirit in the words, 'If any man thirst, let him come unto me, and drink' (Jn. vii. 37). This is the reverse side of what we have been considering in the preceding paragraph. The Spirit will not be given where there is no desire for Him. If men are happy to walk in their own selfish way, if they have no desire to tread the path of lowly service, if they feel no need of divine aid in overcoming the evil within them and in doing the good they in their better moments desire, then there is no gift of the Spirit for them. But if they realize their own short-comings, if they long for the life that is offered them in Christ, if they thirst for the Spirit, if they humbly seek God's good gift, then He will freely grant them His Spirit.

Sometimes the same truth is put otherwise. Peter called on men to repent and be baptized if they would receive the Spirit (Acts ii. 38). Men must turn from every evil way, for the presence of the Spirit is incompatible with a readiness to do evil. The one excludes the other. I read the other day of a small boy who got his hand caught in the neck of a vase. His father tried hard, but without success, to extricate the boy's hand. He did not wish to break the vase, a valuable one, and exhorted his son to one more try. 'Hold your fingers out, quite straight, like this,' he said, 'then pull!' 'But I can't do that, Daddy', retorted his son and heir. 'If I did I'd drop my penny!' The sad thing is that Christians so often hold firmly to their penny, and miss the freedom of the Spirit's fullness.

The New Testament demand for repentance must be set

[1] *Ibid.*

against the religious scene of the day. Jewish religion then was essentially legalistic, a religion of law. Men were busily engaged in heaping up a credit balance of good deeds over bad. To keep on the right side of the ledger was the important thing. A little sin here and there did not matter, as long as there was enough good to set against it. The Christian demand for repentance cut clean across all such attitudes. The believer can never be content to sin so long as the sin remains within decent limits. He must make a clean break with it. He must forsake it utterly. Devotion to regulations must give way to devotion to the living God.

But the forsaking of evil is not everything. Christianity is essentially positive. Christians do the will of God. So Peter and the rest of the apostles can speak of 'the Holy Ghost, whom God hath given to them that obey him' (Acts v. 32). It is the man who places himself in the line of God's will who receives the Spirit. If we will not obey God, we need not expect to receive His Spirit. Obedience, moreover, is a whole-hearted thing. So often we give to God a partial obedience. We do not dare to disobey, but we do not care to obey fully. So we compromise. We do some of what we should, thus removing the stigma of disobedience. But we refrain from the most difficult or objectionable or uncomfortable part, and thus try to get the best of both worlds. Not so will we receive the Spirit of God.

It is no surprise that the gift of the Spirit is sometimes linked with faith, the characteristic Christian attitude. Paul presents this truth with typical vigour in writing to the Galatians. He stigmatizes them as 'foolish' and asks, in a series of rhetorical questions: 'Received ye the Spirit by the works of the law, or by the hearing of faith? Are ye so foolish? having begun in the Spirit, are ye now perfected in the flesh? . . . He therefore that supplieth to you the Spirit, and worketh miracles among you, doeth he it by the works of the law, or by the hearing of faith?' (Gal. iii. 1–5). Clearly faith is the necessary prerequisite to receiving the Spirit. We receive 'the promise of the Spirit through faith' (Gal. iii. 14). Similarly John speaks of the Spirit being given to them 'that believed on him' (Jn. vii. 39).

All this does not mean that a separate specific act of faith is necessary if we are to receive the Spirit, as some have taught. Jack Ford, for example, thinks of the necessity for a time lapse between justification and sanctification. He thinks that justified people should not hurry too quickly into sanctification. He even asks whether people are hustled 'into a profession of holiness before they are sufficiently enlightened and prepared to take the step of faith'.[1] But the scriptural passages dealing with faith and the Spirit point to no such interval (Ford makes no attempt to appeal to Scripture for this point). They are to be interpreted in the light of the other passages we have cited. Paul is outlining the Christian way, and he insists that it is the way of faith and not works. If a man is to receive the Spirit (and without the Spirit he cannot be called a Christian at all, Rom. viii. 9, 14), he must come by the way of faith. When he sincerely trusts Christ for his salvation, then he receives the Spirit of God (cf. Jn. vii. 39). Faith is the gateway to all the blessings that the Christian receives.

Wonderful though the gift of the Spirit is, Scripture makes it clear that there are more wonderful things yet ahead of the believer. Paul can speak of the Spirit as a 'firstfruits' (Rom. viii. 23), and several times he says the Spirit is an 'earnest' (2 Cor. i. 22, v. 5; Eph. i. 14). This last term is practically unintelligible to the modern reader, but the Greek word was luminous to the early believers. It stood for a 'down payment', a first instalment, which was at one and the same time a part of the final sum, and a pledge that the rest would follow. In modern Greek, I am told, the word has come to mean an engagement ring. This is an excellent illustration of what takes place when the Holy Spirit of God is given to the believer, signifying as it does a new relationship already established, but pointing to a grander consummation as yet future. The gift of the Spirit now is a guarantee that there are greater things ahead of the Christian than anything he has yet experienced. The 'down payment' is a pledge that the rest of his inheritance will follow.

---

[1] *What the Holiness People Believe*, Birkenhead, n.d., p. 33.

This has reference partly to this life, and partly to that which is to come. So important is it that Neill Q. Hamilton can maintain that in the New Testament 'the Spirit is related primarily to the future, to eternity, to the time of the consummation of the redemptive process'.[1] This is profoundly important. It means that in the gift of the Spirit the believer receives something of the powers and the life of the world to come. His life in the Spirit is literally 'out of this world'. It is a preview, a foretaste of the blessedness set before us.

OPPOSING THE SPIRIT

If there are certain attitudes we may adopt which open the way to the blessing of the Spirit, there are also certain attitudes which have the contrary effect. It is a great mystery that the creature should be able to assert his petty will against that of the Creator, to turn away from the Spirit's leadings, and in some sense nullify the Divine. Yet the Scripture assures us that this is indeed the case.

Sometimes we read that this terrible possibility has become a reality. Thus Peter castigates Ananias for lying to the Holy Ghost (Acts v. 3), a lie which brought terrible consequences. Again, Stephen boldly maintained that the characteristic sin of his nation, a sin manifested afresh by his persecutors, was that of resisting the Holy Spirit. 'Ye stiffnecked and uncircumcised in heart and ears, ye do always resist the Holy Ghost: as your fathers did, so do ye' (Acts vii. 51). In persecuting those who spoke of Christ, the Jews resisted the very Spirit of God.

Sometimes men are warned of the serious sin it is. Thus we are told in Hebrews that he is worthy of a 'much sorer punishment' than death who among other things 'hath done despite unto the Spirit of grace' (Heb. x. 29). The Spirit is 'the Spirit of grace' because He continually comes to us bringing the gracious gifts of God. He never comes bargaining; always He gives. To reject Him is to reject God in all His graciousness.

[1] *The Holy Spirit and Eschatology in Paul*, Edinburgh (London), 1957, p. 17. The theme is developed throughout the book especially in chapter III.

Paul brings the same point out when he writes to the Thessalonians, 'he that rejecteth, rejecteth not man, but God, who giveth his Holy Spirit unto you' (1 Thes. iv. 8). Paul is dealing with a specific sin (sexual impurity), and he insists that the man who refuses to obey the divine command, the man who engages in this impurity, sins against a God who never ceases to proffer the gift of the Spirit. When he sins, such a man is turning away from the gift that God is offering him at that very moment. It is a vivid way of underlining the seriousness of sin, and it brings out the possibility of man's turning away from the Spirit and rejecting His leadings.

Sometimes the Scripture issues commands on the subject. Two are specially important: 'grieve not the Holy Spirit of God' (Eph. iv. 30), and 'quench not the Spirit' (1 Thes. v. 19). The former of these directs attention to the joyous harmony that ought to exist between the believer and the Spirit of God. Hermas, a second-century Roman writer, has a striking phrase in which he speaks of the Holy Spirit as 'a cheerful Spirit' (*Mand.* x). But it lies within the power of man to grieve this cheerful Spirit. This may be done by engaging in the kind of activity that is alien to the profession of a Christian. The passage in Ephesians mentions such things as bitterness and angry speech, but the expression is capable of a very wide application.

Quenching the Spirit probably does not differ very greatly. The imagery is taken from that of fire. The Holy Spirit is likened to fire, or symbolized by fire, in a number of places and certainly fire may illustrate very aptly some of the work of the Spirit. But conduct like that which Paul is castigating, idleness, impurity, and the like, quenches the Spirit. When a man consents to have such things in his life, then the effective power of the Spirit within him is quenched. The bright burning of the fire of the Spirit and a willingness to engage in sin are absolutely inconsistent with each other.

It is a very solemn thought that God allows men in some degree to thwart His Spirit in this way. It impresses upon us that we must not take the good gift of God for granted. It is well that we reflect on the conditions that Scripture lays down for the effectual working of the Spirit and that we ensure, as far as in us lies, that these conditions are completely fulfilled. God does not view our reaction to the good gift of the Spirit with equanimity. James iv. 5 is a difficult verse, but should probably be understood as RSV, 'Or do you suppose it is in vain that the scripture says, "He yearns jealously over the spirit which he has made to dwell in us"?' On this Tasker comments: 'God is a jealous God who will brook no rivals. It is His Spirit that has been given to the Christian, and He cannot view with anything but jealousy the harbouring by the Christian within his soul of any rival spirit such as the spirit of the world.'[1]

[1] *Tyndale Commentary, in loc.*

CHAPTER IX

CONCLUSION

CLEARLY the doctrine of the Holy Spirit is a very significant doctrine. There are some who maintain that the most important task confronting the Church of today is that of giving adequate definition to this doctrine. There is all the difference in the world between understanding the Spirit as more or less the prisoner of the Church, as one who gives grace *ex opere operato* when the Church wills that the sacraments be performed, and seeing Him as the Lord of the Church, who in sovereign freedom raises up whom He will to be His instrument as He directs the Church into paths of His own choosing. It is important that we be clear in our own minds as to which of these alternatives we espouse, or whether we prefer some other view altogether. Clearly we will not be able to live out our Christian faith without some definite convictions on the relationship of the Spirit to the Church.

It is also important that we think out the relations of the Spirit to the believer. Some very great exegetes have held that the believer's part is simply to be quiescent. 'Let go, and let God' has become a slogan in certain circles. Others point out that in the New Testament believers are far from quiescent. They are very active indeed. The New Testament writers liken the Christian way to a warfare or a race or the like, where strenuous effort is required. Both groups agree that the believer's strength lies in the gift of the Holy Spirit. They differ as to the degree of energy God demands of him.

There is also the question of precisely how the believer is to receive the good gifts of the Spirit. Some think he must go through a spiritual crisis quite distinct from conversion and justification. Others look with grave suspicion on any 'second blessing' in the firm conviction that God has given His good Spirit at the moment of re-birth and that all that is subsequently required of the believer is to make use of the gifts that have been supplied to him.

The scope of this book has meant that we have not been able to go into deep and important questions like these in the detail that we would have wished. Nevertheless we have been able to notice the main outlines of scriptural teaching, and the direction in which solutions are likely to be found. We wish now to emphasize that no Christian is at liberty to evade such questions. He must think them through for himself.

There are two points of especial importance that must receive emphasis. The first of these is that to which we devoted a complete chapter, namely that the Holy Spirit is indeed God. We must not drift into the habit of thinking of Him as no more than a vague force or power or stream or effluence making for good. Nor must we allow ourselves to separate Him from the Father and the Son, outwardly subscribing to all the orthodox formulas, but practically reducing Him to a lower status. The Trinitarian view of the Spirit is absolutely essential. When the Spirit comes into our lives, and gives us a strength not our own, then that is as fully an action of God as it is possible for an action to be. In the Spirit we have access to the infinite divine resources of God Himself. It is imperative that we do not lose sight of the dignity of Him with whom we have to do.

The other point is that God expects all His people to experience to the full all that the indwelling of the Spirit can mean. He has not chosen out a few favoured saints who may enjoy the power of the Spirit as a special enabling, granted to them as an exceptional privilege. He makes the gift of the Spirit available to all. He sets before all the path of Christian service, demanding from everyone the highest possible standard. But He does not leave us staring in hopelessness at what He asks of us. He gives us all the gift of His Spirit, enabling us in a measure to attain that standard.

This is not a dose of spiritual soothing syrup. It is a spiritual dynamic. Wherever there is privilege, there is always corresponding responsibility. And since God has given to us the inestimable privilege of the gift of His Holy Spirit, there lies squarely on our shoulders the responsibility of using His good gift aright.

This, then, is the most practical of doctrines. For an understanding of the nature of God that even approaches being adequate, or for an understanding of the path of Christian service that can be in any degree satisfying, it is imperative that we come to grips with the doctrine of the Spirit.